Colonel John Pelham
LEE'S BOY ARTILLERIST

COLONEL JOHN PELHAM
Courtesy of The Museum of the Confederacy, Richmond, Virginia

William Woods Hassler

COLONEL
John Pelham
LEE'S BOY ARTILLERIST

Illustrations by Sidney E. King

The University of North Carolina Press   Chapel Hill

To Bob and Tom
My Two Twentieth Century Pelhams

CONTENTS

MAPS AND ILLUSTRATIONS

PREFACE

This is the true story of John Pelham—the most beloved and esteemed young man in the Confederacy. His superiors relied on him because he was a brilliant artillerist. His men trusted him because he was fair and considerate. Charming Dixie belles loved him because he was handsome and chivalrous. And the whole South worshipped him because he modestly played a decisive role in victory after victory.

These same qualities which endeared John Pelham to his countrymen a century ago still serve as an inspiration to the youth of today. It is my hope that in the pages of this book readers of all ages may re-live the heroic exploits and breathe the dedicated spirit of this remarkable young man.

William W. Hassler
Willow Grove, Pa.

ACKNOWLEDGEMENTS

One of the most gratifying rewards of writing is the invaluable assistance rendered by interested persons. I wish to acknowledge special appreciation to the following. To Dr. James C. Hazlett of Wheeling, West Virginia for "hard-to-get" information and pictures of the Blakely gun and for tracking down the correct spelling of the name of this English fieldpiece. To Mrs. James S. Patton of Alexandria, Virginia for making available numerous excerpts from her grandmother's diary which provide an intimate insight into Pelham at the time of the Battle of Fredericksburg. To Mr. George Kusel of Willow Grove for helpful guidance on matters pertaining to Civil War arms. To Joseph O'Donnell and Dr. Sidney Forman, archivists of the United States Military Academy, for providing Pelham's record at West Point. To Mr. Sidney E. King, Virginia artist, who combined artistry with a sense of history in drawing the illustrations and maps for the book. To Mr. G. Edmond Massie, with whom it is always a pleasure to work, and whose encouragement and advice are indispensable. And to Mary, my dear and devoted wife, who as usual acted as general editorial assistant and counselor.

CHAPTER I

The Training of a Soldier

In all his seventeen years adventure-loving John Pelham could not remember a year which was nearly as exciting as 1856. Almost every newspaper carried gory accounts of new violence in "Bloody Kansas" where Northern and Southern sympathizers were hustling ruffians into the territory to fight for or against the state's admission into the Union as a slave state.

During May a wild-eyed migrant farmer by the name of John Brown cruelly murdered five pro-slavery Kansas settlers along Pottawatomie Creek. In Washington, Representative Preston Brooks of South Carolina angrily strode into the Senate chamber and, without warning, clubbed Senator John Sumner of Massachusetts with his cane until the anti-slavery New Englander fell unconscious beside the desk at which he had been working quietly.

In his own state of Alabama, John listened to bitter stories about William Strickland and Edwin Upson, owners of the largest bookstore in downstate Mobile. These two storekeepers had been run out of town by enraged citizens because they sold three anti-slavery books which some curious customers had ordered. Dr. Pelham cautioned his boys to keep calm in the hope that passions would cool. But when Major Buford of South Carolina stopped in Alabama to recruit several hundred daring lads who could handle a musket, John Pelham itched to join the crusade which was heading for Kansas under a blazing red banner bearing the motto "SOUTH CAROLINA AND STATES' RIGHTS."

However, John wisely decided to follow his father's advice and first obtain an education at the United States Military Academy at West Point. Certainly no young man had a better background to recommend him for such an appointment. He was the third son of Dr. Atkinson Pelham and his wife Martha, both prominent citizens of Benton County in northeastern Alabama. Here on a thousand acre estate young John and his five brothers played their share of pranks and became embroiled in rough scrapes. "Those wild Pelham boys", as the neighbors called them, always seemed to be up to some mischief or other. They played hooky from school to fish and hunt; they feasted on farmers' ripe corn and luscious melons; and they deviled their teacher by removing and hiding all the desks in the little one-room schoolhouse.

In this healthy outdoor environment John Pelham developed a wiry athletic physique which later enabled him to endure strenuous battle campaigning with such sturdy veterans as Generals Robert E. Lee, "Stonewall" Jackson, and "Jeb" Stuart. The young Alabamian enjoyed all sports and rough-and-tumble activities. When he and his brothers tired of fighting each other they would tussle with anyone who was spoiling for a fight. On one such occasion John took on a scrapper much larger than himself. Pelham fought gamely, but he soon realized that he was no match for the older lad who battered him so hard that Charlie, John's oldest brother, started to step in and take his kid brother's part. But John waved him back, shouting, "No, Charlie, I'll fight this one out myself." And slug it out he did until he fell to the ground completely exhausted.

Another favorite sport of John's was horseback riding in which he became expert at an early age. When he tired of riding horses across the cotton fields he rode a neighbor's cow around the pasture. Several days of this vigorous exercise reduced the poor cow and cut her milk supply to a trickle. Pelham then went to the irate owner and admitted that he was responsible for the cow's rundown condition. The farmer ordered John hereafter to leave the cows alone and ride the bull if he felt he must ride some animal beside a horse for variety. This idea appealed immensely to Pelham who proceeded to mount the bull which snorted unhappily as it pranced back and forth in a furious attempt to dislodge the determined rider. But Pelham stayed on and eventually tamed the bull so that even his younger sister Betty could ride him.

But now that the country was seething with internal troubles, seventeen year old John Pelham put aside these fun-loving antics to seriously consider his future. During the national crisis of 1856 John and his father talked with the Honorable S. W. Harris, local representative to the United States Congress, about the possibility of securing an appointment for John to attend West Point. Congressman Harris was favorably impressed by young Pelham's sincerity and manliness, and promptly obtained the appointment for him.

The last week in June John bade farewell to his family and started north to this country's best school for military training and engineering. On the last leg of his journey he took the leisurely steamboat ride from New York to West Point. Upon leaving the boat at the South Dock pier he climbed with his bags up the steep slopes to the broad and remarkably flat plain

which commands a panoramic view of the peaceful Hudson
and the majestic heights bordering the opposite shore.

In the middle of the plain stood a group of two, three and
four-storied buildings which housed the offices, classrooms and
barracks. A cadet sergeant directed John to the administration
building where he signed the register and was immediately
assigned to Company D which was composed mostly of Southern boys. Pelham shared his cramped quarters with Tom
Rosser, a tall, powerfully built Virginian whom John soon
came to admire and respect. Another classmate with whom
John formed a close and warm friendship was Adelburt Ames
of Maine who later remembered Pelham as "easily the most
popular man of the Corps . . . everybody liked him." Ames
himself later became a "boy general" in the Union army.

"Plebe" Pelham entered West Point under an experimental
five-year program established by Jefferson Davis in 1854 when
he was Secretary of War under President Pierce. July and
August the new students or "plebes" got their first taste of
army life as they encamped on the Plain. Throughout the hot
summer days these future officers "fell in" shortly after daybreak for inspection, followed by long hours of drilling in
infantry tactics and artillery practice. While most of the sweating youths dropped off to sleep at the end of each day—four
in a tent—a few classmates took turns standing guard on the
post. These sentinels were frequently the butt of upper-class-
men, who would wrap themselves in sheets and approach the
guards on hands and knees while muttering strange words
which scared the new "plebes" into believing they were being
challenged by weird creatures from outer space. But in spite
of the rugged schedule and teasings, most of the "plebes" including Pelham came to enjoy this outdoor experience more
than any other at the Academy.

When the hardened "plebes" returned to barracks in September they plunged into the study of mathematics and English. John was bright and enjoyed reading entertaining adventure books, but he did not study as much as either he or his instructors knew he should. Sometimes he would put off studying until too near the deadline. Then he had to tack blankets over his window in order to study after taps sounded lights out at 10 o'clock. Although he was by no means a model student, Pelham managed to pass the oral final examinations and finish 35th in a class of 59.

In contrast to his mediocre work in his studies, John excelled in cavalry tactics and athletics. Every afternoon he practiced riding on the cavalry plain, followed in the evening by an hour's boxing and fencing in the gymnasium. Despite his medium build, John shortly gained the reputation of being the finest athlete at the Academy. When the Prince of Wales visited West Point in 1860, the future King Edward VII of England was impressed by the form and grace of Cadet Pelham's horsemanship. For years after Pelham left the Academy, instructors and cadets held up his riding feats as a model to imitate.

John's athletic ability coupled with his friendliness and integrity made him a favorite among his classmates. When he tried out for the color-guard (an honor that required military bearing plus "spit and polish") his fellow cadets made sure that he was perfectly garbed in every detail. One classmate loaned him a new waist-belt, another brought a gleaming scabbard, while still a third carefully whisked the last specks of dust from Pelham's gun. During this ceremony the modest Alabamian, blushingly thanked his friends for their attention and help, but said he didn't think he'd get the position. However, the regular army officers at the Academy thought otherwise and appointed him to the post from which he later advanced to a cadet non-commissioned officer and finally to a cadet officer.

Cadet Pelham was just as particular about his habits off the parade ground as on. When the distinguished Board of Visitors inspected the Academy in 1860 the president of the Board personally complimented Pelham on the neatness and cleanliness of his room, jokingly adding that Pelham had no need of a wife as he could keep an orderly house by himself. And when a number of cadets were caught and arrested for drunkenness, John wrote disgustedly to his father: "None of these cadets were members of the first or second classes, of course, for we are on a pledge to abstain from all intoxicating liquors."

For recreation the cadets had to rely on their own ingenuity as there were no movies, radio or television in Pelham's day. In fact, the only opportunity John had to visit his family occurred at the end of his second year when his class was granted a two-month furlough. Nevertheless, Pelham and his classmates contrived to fill their few leisure hours reading, writing letters, and dancing. They usually danced with each other during the winter months as West Point was too isolated for visits from the fairer sex.

However, in the summer months attractive young ladies in bright crinoline dresses and parasols swarmed to the "Point" hoping to make the acquaintance of the smartly uniformed handsome cadets. Although Cadet Pelham belonged to the Bachelors' Club because he believed a young man should not become serious with a girl until he was in a position to get married, he nevertheless enjoyed viewing through a telescope the colorful parade of beauties who promenaded on the walks bordering the green Plain.

During Pelham's third summer at the Academy rumors began circulating throughout the barracks that the blond, blue-eyed Alabamian was deserting the Bachelor's Club to date a sweet fair lady from nearby Newburgh. When John confirmed the gossip, he was roundly teased by his classmates who taunted him on his way to meet his date with cries of: "Look here, fellows, Pelham has turned ladies man . . ."

For more serious recreation Pelham took an active interest in the Dialectic Society which was devoted to the study and discussion of important current issues. When he was elected president of this organization John proudly wrote his mother: "I am getting on very well."

With the election of Abraham Lincoln as President of the United States in the fall of 1860, Pelham found himself presiding over heated discussions of slavery and states' rights at the meetings of the Dialectic Society. Considerable feeling was sparked at the Academy by a straw vote in which only 64 of the 210 cadets voted for Lincoln. A group of staunch Southerners began campaigning against "the Black Republican Abolitionists in the Corps." Despite some bitter name calling on both sides, Pelham and a number of other level-headed cadets calmed tempers by showing respect for each other's convictions. In a patriotic address to the entire cadet body Cadet Bill McCreery, a good friend of Pelham's, called for an end to angry North South rivalry in these healing words: "Let us put from us the seeds of sectional strife and draw closer and closer the bonds of this glorious union."

Unfortunately, this sensible attitude was not shared by powerful national political hotheads on both sides who kept the slavery issue boiling. Cadet Pelham viewed with alarm the rush of events pushing the country toward war. Like many Southern cadets at the Academy he was torn between loyalty to his country and devotion to his state. He had made many friends among his Northern classmates, and he recalled local political rallies back in his native Alexandria at which his father had argued against bellowing secessionists who wanted to withdraw from the Union. On the other hand he put his loyalty to his native state first, and on this basis he sadly but definitely decided to cast his lot with whatever course his beloved state of Alabama took. Shortly before Christmas in 1860 he described his mixed feelings in a letter to his mother:

My dear Mother,

You can't imagine how glad I was to get a letter from you—I had been looking for it for a long, long time. You may expect to see me home by the first of February, 1861. I regret the circumstances which make it necessary, but I don't see any remedy. Alabama seems determined to leave the Union before the middle of January, and I think it would be dishonorable in me to withhold my services when they will be needed. It seems pretty hard that I should toil for four and a half years for a diploma and then have to leave without it. I am studying hard and think I shall be higher after the coming January examinations than I have ever been before; but my standing will not do me any good.

I always (nearly always) get over my lessons and read a chapter in my Bible a short time before eleven at night. I am not allowed to have a light after this hour. For the past two years and a half I have read my Bible regularly, one chapter almost every night; and when I neglected it one night I made it up the next. I must write a short note to father tonight.

Lovingly your son,
John

When Alabama passed an Ordinance of Secession on January 11, 1861, Cadet John Pelham did not immediately follow either his own plans or the advice of his native politicians to resign from the Academy and offer his sword to the Cotton State. Instead, he stayed on hoping that somehow he might be able to graduate before the fighting began. His hope was strengthened somewhat in January when Major Pierre G. T. Beauregard of Louisiana replaced Major Richard Delafield as Superintendent of the Academy. Major Beauregard, or "Old Bory" as the cadets nicknamed him, advised the Southern cadets to remain in the regular army as long as he did, but after only five days he was dismissed from his post.

During February and March a number of Southern boys resigned, but Pelham stayed on until the Academy received the jarring news of a sharp artillery engagement at Fort Sumter on April 12th and 13th. According to newspaper accounts, Southern artillerists under the command of Brigadier General Beauregard (who had resigned from the U. S. Army shortly after he was dismissed from his post at the Academy), had bombarded Fort Sumter, a United States fort located in the harbor of Charleston, South Carolina. The newly formed Confederate government had ordered General Beauregard to destroy the fort because President Lincoln was sending a fleet with supplies for the small garrison. After a furious two-day shelling by Confederate batteries, Major Robert Anderson (who had taught artillery tactics to General Beauregard years before at West Point) surrendered his command of sixty-seven soldiers and officers together with a band of thirteen musicians.

The fall of Fort Sumter immediately split the cadet corps at the Academy into two hostile camps. The Northern cadets held a loud rally at which rabid speeches were made followed by a rousing singing of The Star Spangled Banner. The vastly outnumbered Southern boys made no demonstrations but kept to their quarters. Pelham now realized that he must leave, particularly as there was now heated talk of holding Southern cadets as prisoners of war.

Two weeks before graduation Pelham and Tom Rosser quietly slipped away from the Academy and headed west to avoid possible capture and punishment by the inflamed citizens in the metropolitan cities through which the cadets normally passed en route to their Southern homes. The round-about journey put a strain on the boys' resources as the Academy had withheld their pay since December.

Nevertheless, the two Southern patriots encountered no difficulties on their swift trip until they reached New Albany, Indiana just across the Ohio River from Kentucky—and freedom. Here the authorities detained the uniformed pair to inquire what two West Point cadets were doing in Indiana. Thinking quickly, Pelham replied that they were couriers on an important mission for General Winfield S. Scott, Commander-in-Chief of the United States Army. Impressed and satisfied, the officers released the youthful "couriers".

Making their way to nearby Jeffersonville, John and Tom were confronted with the problem of getting across the Ohio River without attracting the attention of local guards patrolling the banks. As Alabama was at war, Pelham used a ruse he would not have thought of using in peacetime. He flirted with a young Indiana maiden who was instantly captivated by the cadet's handsomeness and gallant manners. He persuaded her to row him and his husky companion across the river to the Kentucky shore. There he hastily bade farewell to his admirer and the pair struck south toward Alabama.

CHAPTER II

Turning the Tide at Manassas (Bull Run)

J OHN PELHAM's homecoming was the occasion for a traditional Southern celebration. A suckling pig was barbecued on the outdoor spit, and as the family and friends enjoyed delicious ham they plied John and Tom with questions about their exciting experiences in eluding the Federal authorities en route to Alabama. John modestly related their adventures, adding that his greatest thrill was to be home again after an absence of almost three years. Tom said he too was glad to be on Southern soil again, although his own state of Virginia had not yet seceded.

When word spread that young Pelham had returned home, folks started dropping in to welcome him back and to inquire about conditions in the North. Everyone was excited about the conflict, and John and Tom needed no urging to offer their services to the local authorities. For the next few weeks in May the two West Pointers drilled the raw volunteers in the nearby town of Jacksonville.

Meanwhile more states were joining the Confederacy whose government headed by President Jefferson Davis was meeting in the temporary capital of Montgomery, Alabama. Before the government moved into its permanent headquarters in Richmond, Virginia late in May, Tom and John traveled to Montgomery to report for duty. As West Pointers were urgently needed to officer the new gray-uniformed army being hurriedly organized, both boys were commissioned lieutenants in the Confederate service. Rosser was assigned to coastal duty in North Carolina while Pelham was ordered to take charge of Confederate ordnance at Lynchburg, Virginia.

Lieutenant Pelham arrived in Lynchburg the end of May and proceeded to direct the assembling, repair, and distribution of arms and ammunition. Although he realized the importance of this ordnance work and performed his duties efficiently, Pelham yearned for action on the fighting front. Hence he was jubilant when the June mails brought orders from the War Department in Richmond directing him to report for active duty with General Joseph E. Johnston's Army of the Shenandoah encamped near Winchester, gateway to the fertile farmlands of the Shenandoah Valley.

Just before Pelham's arrival General Johnston had withdrawn his small army of 7,000 inexperienced recruits from Harper's Ferry to Winchester in order to block General Robert Patterson's 18,000 ninety-day volunteers from crossing the Potomac River and occupying the Shenandoah Valley. Able General Johnston, a short, quiet commander with a pointed goatee was busily engaged in whipping his outnumbered force into fighting form. Assisting him was Colonel Thomas J. Jackson, ex-professor of mathematics at Virginia Military Institute. From the soldiers Pelham heard fantastic stories about Colonel Jackson's peculiar habits—how he liked to suck lemons as he sat thoughtfully on his horse, Little Sorrel; how he preferred to wear dingy, baggy uniforms instead of the fancy gold-braided styles worn by most officers; and how he insisted on his officers attending church and prayer services at which he invariably went to sleep. Despite the Colonel's odd traits, Pelham soon came to admire him immensely because "Old Jack", as the men affectionately called him, was a man of few words, a strict disciplinarian, and most of all he was spoiling for a fight with the Yankees.

Another of General Johnston's officers who quickly earned Pelham's respect was Lieutenant-Colonel "Jeb" Stuart, a dashing and fearless red-bearded cavalryman who was always scouting the enemy's position. "Jeb" was a large man with boundless energy and nerves that never seemed to tire. In his cavalier hat he always wore a black ostrich plume which waved in the breeze as he gaily chanted the song "Jine the Cavalry" while Sam Sweeney, his aide, strummed the tune on his banjo.

Upon reporting to General Johnston at army headquarters, Lieutenant Pelham was assigned to Captain Ephraim Alburtis' battery as drillmaster. Captain Alburtis, an elderly officer from nearby Martinsburg, was surprised to find that his new aide was a soldierly-looking beardless boy. But Pelham quickly dispelled any doubts his superior may have had concerning his ability and behavior. Instead of acting like a young upstart, Pelham showed complete respect for Captain Alburtis' authority and executed all of his orders with dispatch.

Pelham in turn was surprised on meeting and inspecting his command to discover that they were dressed in uniforms of all descriptions provided by the various states which they represented. In addition to soldiers from his own state of Alabama, Lieutenant Pelham counted volunteers from Virginia, Maryland, the Carolinas, Georgia, Tennessee, and Mississippi.

Although Pelham's sixty-two recruits were undisciplined and knew nothing whatsoever about cannons, they were eager to learn. And teach them Pelham did, even though he had only four outdated smooth-bore six-pounder guns some of which lacked horses to pull them, caissons in which to store ammunition, and limbers or mounted chests for the tools needed to fire the cannon. Undaunted, Pelham sweated side-by-side with his soldiers to convert old crates and ammunition boxes into caissons and limbers. Meanwhile, "Jeb" Stuart managed to "borrow" several teams of enemy horses to haul the battery's guns, ammunition, and paraphernalia.

Within a month Lieutenant Pelham's rugged daily routine had transformed Captain Alburtis' battery from an awkward squad into the most polished gunnery unit in General Johnston's army. At Pelham's order the cannoneers responded with machine-like precision as they loaded, rammed, aimed and fired the cannon, after which the hot barrel was cooled and sparks extinguished with a sponge attached to the end of a long pole. Before long the dash and skill of this battery attracted admiring crowds among whom were Colonels Jackson and Stuart who inquired the name of the forceful boy leader.

On July Fourth Pelham thought for a while that he might have an opportunity to show what his boys could do in battle. Early in the morning the boom of heavy guns roared from the Federal camp at Martinsburg about twenty miles away. General Johnston first thought that General Patterson was laying down a heavy artillery barrage preparatory to launching an all-out assault. At General Johnston's order the Confederate infantrymen rushed to take their places in line while Pelham's artillerists loaded the cannons. But when the bluecoats showed no disposition to move, a Confederate flag-bearer shouted: "The Yanks are just celebrating Independence Day."

He was right. Unfortunately, ammunition in Johnston's army was too scarce for Pelham's guns to answer with a salute honoring the independence they were now fighting to win. Instead,

General Johnston ordered the regimental bands to strike up "Dixie" from one end of the line to the other.

While Pelham and his men waited impatiently each day for the Army of the Shenandoah to march against the enemy so that they could "shoot the Yankees, get the war over, and go home," events were fast moving to a climax on the Washington side of the Blue Ridge Mountains. At Manassas, a tiny but vital railroad junction sixty miles east of Winchester and twenty-five miles west of Washington, General Pierre Beauregard, the hero of Fort Sumter, was frantically trying to organize and train a force to bar General Irvin McDowell's Union army from marching through northern Virginia and capturing Richmond, new capital of the Confederacy.

Every day the Confederates received reports of General McDowell's growing army which was encamped just outside Washington. By the middle of July the U.S. capital was overflowing with excitement as orderlies on horseback raced with messages from government officials to generals and back again; soldiers donned their gold-braided blue uniforms and polished their muskets and bayonets; and everyone in the District of Columbia talked confidently about ending the war by the Grand Army's "On to Richmond" drive.

One spectator who observed these proceedings with intense interest from her home near the White House was Mrs. Rose O'Neal Greenhow of the Confederate Secret Service. On July 16 she obtained a copy of the War Department's orders directing plump General McDowell "to move on Manassas tonight." Hastily the middle-aged woman spy scribbled this important news in code on a small slip of paper which she carefully tucked beneath the flowing blonde hair of her young Maryland friend, Betty Duvall.

This adventurous maiden, disguised as a farm woman, passed through the Union picket lines and made a bee-line to the Confederate army at Manassas where she delivered the note. General Beauregard immediately notified President Davis of the impending danger, and the worried President telegraphed General Johnston to give General Patterson the slip at Winchester and hurry to join General Beauregard at Manassas.

At daybreak on Thursday, July 18, General Johnston grimly issued orders for the Army of the Shenandoah to cook three days rations and prepare to break camp at noon. Lieutenant Pelham promptly had his men load the caissons and hitch up the cannons and limbers for what he and his gunners hoped would be a thrilling battle with the enemy.

Therefore, when the army headed south as though retreating from General Patterson's force, the disappointed Confederates began to grumble that they hadn't joined up to run away from Yankees. Pelham also was disturbed by the direction in which the troops were moving, but he had learned at West Point to accept orders and make the best of them. His attitude was rewarded, for as soon as the army got out of earshot of Union spies in Winchester, General Johnston halted the column while officers opened blue envelopes and read the commanding General's order of the day:

"Our gallant army under General Beauregard is now being attacked in overwhelming numbers. The commanding general (General Johnston) hopes that his army will step out like men, and make a forced march to save the country."

At the close of this stirring appeal cheers went up all along the line, and none shouted more wildly than Lieutenant John Pelham of Alabama. With faces now grinning the light-hearted marchers turned east and doubled their pace. About midnight the advance units passed through the majestic Blue Ridge Mountains at Ashby's Gap and bivouacked on the eastern slopes. The twenty-mile march had been a gruelling experience for these untried soldiers, and they dropped off to sleep where they fell.

Before retiring Lieutenant Pelham walked the rounds to make sure sentinels had been posted to prevent a surprise attack. Finding none, he reported the fact to General Jackson who was leaning against a tree thoughtfully sucking a lemon. The newly-promoted General thanked Pelham for his careful attention to duty, and said, "Let the poor fellows sleep, I will guard the camp myself."

Next morning Pelham and his gunners marched beside their cannons to Piedmont Station where they parted company with the footsore infantry that boarded a long line of rickety freight cars on the Manassas Gap Railroad. As the crowded trains pulled out for Manassas the relieved passengers called out to the forlorn gunners, "Get smaller guns and you can ride too."

Fortunately the artillery was accompanied by "Jeb" Stuart and his cavalry which acted as a screen to protect the guns against raiding parties. The cavalry chief struck up an acquaintance with Pelham as they rode at the head of the column. And when Pelham's gun carriages got stuck in the mud, Stuart's troopers galloped up to help pull them out.

When the five batteries of General Johnston's army reached Salem on Saturday morning the cannoneers were warmly greeted by admiring youngsters and flirtatious belles in calico bearing trays of delicious home-cooked goodies and lemonade. Pelham, being young and handsome, naturally attracted more than his share of "waitresses" causing him to blush with embarrassment. His men jokingly told him that they would not vote for him at the next election of officers* if he continued to monopolize all of the beauties everywhere they stopped.

For many soldiers this luscious food, prepared and served by such delicate hands, was to be their last home-cooked meal.

---

*Strange as it seems today, the Confederate soldiers actually did elect their officers!

Leaving Salem the column plodded over hilly ground to White Plains and Hay Market. Late that night they reached the plains of Manassas near the railroad junction. Although it was too dark for Pelham to get a clear view of the terrain, the sparks from thousands of smoldering campfires thrilled him with the knowledge that two major armies were about to lock horns in battle.

Pelham had not slept long on the hard, dry ground when he was roused by a courier who handed him a note. Rubbing his eyes in the dim dawn of a bright Sabbath, Pelham focussed his eyes on the order which directed him to assume command of Captain Alburtis' battery as the older officer was too ill to take the field. Proud of his new responsibility, Lieutenant Pelham notified his men that he would lead them today. Then he ordered them to hitch up the guns, caissons and limbers so that the battery could move on a moment's notice.

Before long Pelham espied Generals Johnston and Beauregard galloping to a nearby hill at Mitchell's Ford where they dismounted and observed the enemy through field glasses. Pelham had not seen "Old Bory" since his short term as Commandant of West Point. This sunny morning the little General looked like a tired and worried Napoleon in his dusty gray uniform. He had been up all night devising plans for the defeat of his former West Point classmate, General Irvin McDowell.

General Johnston, as the highest ranking officer on the field, approved General Beauregard's strategy, following which the two officers now inspected their lines. The battle-front extended a distance of eight miles along a lazy winding stream known as Bull Run. On the Confederate left "Old Bory" had scattered only a few troops to guard the fords and bridges, while he concentrated most of his 32,000 soldiers on the right near Manassas for an offensive he trusted would annihilate the "Grand Army's" 35,000 bluecoats.

But before the Confederates could mount their attack on the right, General McDowell took half of his army on a wide flanking march and fiercely assailed General Beauregard's left at dawn. When the crackle of musketry and the roar of cannon from this sector reached "Old Bory's" ears he rushed reinforcements to stave off a rout.

On receiving his orders to strengthen the left, Lieutenant Pelham ordered his waiting battery: "To horse! Trot!" and away they dashed. Many gunners hitched rides on the caissons and limbers which they hugged with both hands as the carriages jounced over the rough dirt road. On the way they heard the whine of Minié balls which clipped oak leaves and shattered fence rails causing one witty Irishman to exclaim: "Old Abe's splittin' rails agin."

Further on Pelham slackened his pace slightly to avoid hitting the stream of wounded and horribly mangled Confederate soldiers who were hobbling to the rear at the same time they tried to bandage their wounds with handkerchiefs and torn shirts.

When the column neared its destination it slowed to a walk and turned right up an incline overgrown with scrub pines. On the slope the procession passed a two-story frame house belonging to a bed-ridden eighty-five year-old widow, Mrs. Henry, who shortly thereafter was killed by crossfire. At the top of the hill was a broad plateau on the far side of which stood a wooden shanty belonging to a free Negro named Jim Robinson. Bordering the eastern side of the plateau was a fringe of pine thickets in front of which Pelham caught sight of General Jackson calmly walking his horse as his Virginia Brigade, 3,000 strong, formed in line of battle facing the enemy to the west.

Turning his gaze from the Virginians to the left, Pelham

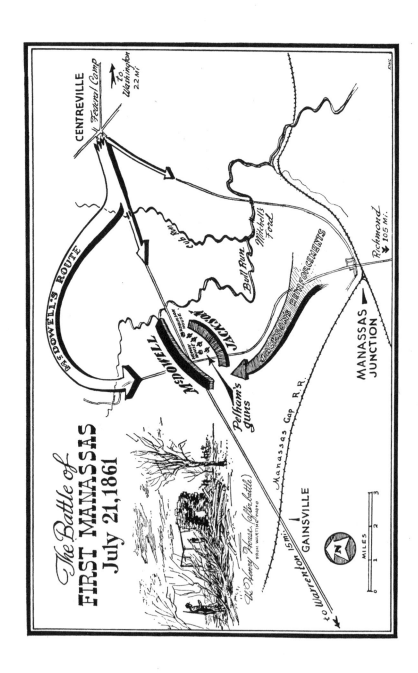

The Battle of
FIRST MANASSAS
July 21, 1861

CENTREVILLE
Federal Camp
To Washington 22 Mi.

McDOWELL'S ROUTE

Cub Run

Bull Run

Mitchell's Ford

JACKSON

McDOWELL

Pelham's guns

JACKSON'S REINFORCEMENTS

Richmond 105 Mi.

MANASSAS JUNCTION

Manassas Gap R.R.

GAINSVILLE

to Warrenton 15 mi.

The Henry House (after battle)
FROM WARTIME PHOTO

MILES
0 1 2 3

KING

GENERAL ROBERT E. LEE

A British observer with the Confederate Army described General Lee as "the handsomest man of his age I ever saw . . . tall, broad-shouldered —a thorough soldier in appearance. . . . He is a perfect gentleman in every respect. I imagine no man has so few enemies, or is so universally esteemed."

LIEUTENANT GENERAL T. J. ("STONEWALL") JACKSON

Stern and taciturn, "Stonewall" planned his next move in the saddle while sucking on a lemon. General Lee called him his "right arm" and claimed that "the sun never shone on such an executive officer."

pursed his lips in determination as he viewed the brave Confederate brigades of General Bartow, Bee and Evans being forced back by what appeared to be endless waves of bluecoats supported by about twenty guns. The young artillerist immediately wheeled Alburtis' battery into position in front of General Jackson's right near the Robinson house.

As soon as the cannons were loaded, Pelham sighted them and coolly ordered his sweating gunners to "Fire!" As the four guns barked Pelham observed their effect and corrected the aim and range when necessary. Soon the battery was delivering a furious fire which mowed down the advancing bluecoats, slowed their advance and gave the thin gray line an opportunity to break off the action and retire to a new position.

Before long the graycoats were streaming up the slopes toward the plateau pursued closely by the Federals who paused only long enough to fire their volleys. When General Bee saw General Jackson's brigade lined up shoulder-to-shoulder, he pointed his sword toward the Virginia brigade and shouted to his scattered and demoralized troops: "There stands Jackson like a stone wall. Rally behind the Virginians." Thereafter, General Jackson was called "Stonewall" by his admiring soldiers.

It was now early in the afternoon, and as 6,000 Confederates courageously fought to ward off defeat at the hands of 11,000 Federals on Henry House Hill (as the plateau was called), General Beauregard and General McDowell personally took command of the opposing forces. For two hours the battle seesawed back and forth on the plain with the blue and gray lines charging and countercharging. Two of General McDowell's most destructive batteries advanced close to the Confederate lines to pour a heavy fire at point-blank range, whereupon "Jeb" Stuart gayly stampeded the gunners while "Stonewall" Jackson's Thirty-third Virginia Regiment ran forward and captured the guns. These batteries subsequently changed hands several times, each capturing squad turning them upon the enemy.

All this time Lieutenant John Pelham was calmly directing the steady fire of his field pieces which rained a withering fire on the blue ranks. During a murderous enemy counterattack, General Jackson ordered all batteries to the rear. Bearing a dejected, grimy countenance, Pelham helped his crew haul back the cannon from the edge of the plateau. While thus engaged in taking his battery out of the fight, Pelham glanced back over his shoulder and noticed that Colonel William T. Sherman's bluecoated brigade was stealthily emerging from a hollow to attack "Stonewall's" undefended right flank. Realizing that an unexpected attack from this quarter could shatter the last hope of a Confederate stand, Pelham exclaimed: "I'll be dogged if I'm going any further back."

Whereupon he gamely wheeled his Napoleon cannons into battery and fired directly into the midst of Colonel Sherman's charging regiments. As Pelham's canister shells spewed destruction among the flanking force the broken ranks quickly withdrew. Pelham then proudly patted his gunners and shouted: "Well done, well done. You've beaten off the threat to General Jackson's flank."

By mid-afternoon the exhausted soldiers, having fought for hours under the scorching July sun, paused as if by mutual agreement to catch their breath and gulp a swig of water from dusty canteens. During this lull General Beauregard drew rein in front of his lines. Rising in his stirrups he declared dramatically:

"Comrades, you must hold your ground until reinforcements arrive. Then we will drive the enemy away from our beloved homes and soil. Soldiers of the Confederacy, let us here conquer or die!"

For an hour after the battle was resumed the tide wavered back and forth again. Then at 4 o'clock a column of dust appeared in the sky to the southwest. Soldiers and officers of both armies anxiously asked the same question: Is the approaching force General Patterson's army from Winchester, or Confederate reinforcements? Fearful that it was Patterson's force, "Old Bory" summoned his buglers to sound the retreat. But just as the buglers raised their horns to blow, a light summer breeze caught the banner at the head of the advancing column and unfurled the Virginia flag of General Early's brigade.

Quickly the fresh Confederate reinforcements fell upon the enemy's exposed right flank and rolled it back. General Beauregard, seeing his opportunity for a smashing victory, ordered a general advance all along the line which quickly reeled back General McDowell's army.

The brave Federal commander attempted to rally his fleeing troops, but Pelham's guns and "Stonewall's" batteries shattered each rally with a shower of grapeshot. When the gunners got the range of the stampeding Yankee supply wagons, the Napoleon's cannoneers landed a direct hit on a wagon scurrying across a narrow bridge over Cub Run. Thereupon the horse-drawn vehicle capsized and blocked the bridge to further traffic. This panicked the retreating bluecoats who cast aside their canteens, knapsacks and even their rifles in a mad scramble to escape from the cheering graycoats who screeched the eerie "Ee ow ow ow" that henceforth was famous as the "Rebel Yell."

Lieutenant Pelham jubilantly joined in shouting the new battle cry as he hitched up his guns, now almost down to their last round of ammunition, to join in the chase. But darkness soon ended pursuit, and it was not resumed the next day because heavy rains turned the roads into muddy lanes.

Although Pelham was keenly disappointed that the victorious

Confederate army was unable to capture Washington and end the war at once, he took pride in reports that Generals Johnston, Beauregard and Jackson together with Colonel Stuart had all commented on his brave and skillful handling of Alburtis' battery during this touch-and-go battle of First Manassas or Bull Run. General "Stonewall" Jackson, who seldom praised his officers, undoubtedly had Pelham in mind when he wrote in his official report of the battle: "Nobly did the artillery maintain its position for hours against the enemy's advancing thousands."

The Alabama boy who was to become the greatest artillerist in the Confederacy had passed through his baptism of fire with distinction, glory, and the loss of only two men.

"Bringing off the guns"

Moving up

CHAPTER III

The Horse Artillery Wins Its Spurs

AFTER THE BATTLE of First Manassas General Joseph Johnston's troops pitched camp on the field they had so narrowly won. Meanwhile, the cavalry under "Jeb" Stuart ranged eastward to keep tabs on the demoralized Union army which was catching its breath in the outskirts of Washington. "Jeb," who was promoted from Colonel to Brigadier General for his outstanding service at Bull Run, operated so effectively as the eyes and ears of the Confederate army that General Johnston appreciatively inquired: "How can I eat, sleep or rest without you upon the outpost?"

In the fall of 1861 General Johnston recommended that Pelham be promoted to Captain and transferred to General Stuart's command for a special assignment—the organization of a mobile artillery unit which was to become world-famous as the Stuart Horse Artillery. During the Battle of First Manassas General Stuart had been impressed with the immense advantage that could be gained by rushing cannons to a vital sector where the guns could pour a concentrated fire against enemy troops and artillery. He felt that the best way to accomplish this would be to mount his crews and hitch the cannon to horses that could gallop quickly from one part of the battlefield to another as the battle situation demanded—a tactic that was widely used in the French army.

Pelham eagerly accepted this challenging new assignment even though it meant starting from scratch again to build the organization. As there was no draft during the early days of the war he had to recruit his horse artillerymen from volunteers. Starting with Grove's battery from Culpeper, Virginia, Pelham gradually built his company of twelve commissioned officers and 150 men by "borrowing" troopers from General Stuart's cavalry and enlisting about forty fellow Alabamians who caught his patriotic spirit when he visited his home state on a furlough in the autumn of 1861. Many of these carefree followers were Creoles who lustily sang the French national anthem, the "Marseillaise", as they learned to load and fire the Horse Artillery's new 12-pounder Napoleon gun. Pelham called these industrious boys his "Napoleon Detachment." One of the Creoles to whom Pelham became fondly attached was a tiny energetic chap named Jean who worked furiously as a "sponger" on the Napoleon gun. When Pelham would ask him what he was doing, the black-haired boy replied: "Me, I cool zee Napoleon gun and put out zee sparks after she go boom."

Pelham had as his chief assistant First Lieutenant Jim Breathed, a Virginian who had fought gallantly at Bull Run. Pelham and Breathed divided the men into groups of twenty-five (including eleven cannoneers) for each gun. Then they trained the crews to master the art of hitching concentrated firepower of the artillery to the mobility of horses. Pelham cheerfully but firmly drilled each unit until his men felt as much at home on a horse as they did on foot and could run through their duties blindfolded. Pelham emphasized the importance of teamwork which he said was essential for fast, smooth coordination of every operation involved in rushing the

guns into the right position at the right time to deliver a murderous fire.

Pelham's thorough training and rigorous discipline soon paid dividends in offsetting the Union army's superior artillery, both in numbers and firepower. At the outset the Horse Artillery had only six smooth-bore muzzle-loading brass cannon and three-inch guns having a range of about one mile. But Pelham drilled and led his men so well that he was frequently able to hold his own against heavy odds with only a single gun, and in over sixty fights he never lost a piece of artillery!

On making his daily round of the camps, "Jeb" Stuart usually stopped to observe Pelham check the range and direct the fire of his gunners, after which the commander of the Horse Artillery barked the command: "Limber! Rear! Gallop!" and away the two-wheeled carriages and crews would dash to another practice position.

Stuart smiled admiringly at the way Pelham was rapidly developing this technique. In a letter to his wife General Stuart wrote: "The Horse Battery under the energetic management of Pelham is going ahead and will tell a tale in the next battle."

During the fall and winter (1861-62) that the Confederate forces spent in Northern Virginia preparing for the spring campaign, "Jeb" Stuart and John Pelham became fast friends. Stuart, being five years older and senior in rank, treated Pelham like a kid brother. Their personalities dove-tailed together perfectly. Stuart was an adventurous out-going officer who liked to show off before pretty young ladies whom he would obligingly kiss in public. Pelham also was optimistic in disposition, but he was retiring and modest in front of both men and women. Even though the new mobile artillery unit was directly under his command, he persisted in calling it the Stuart Horse Artillery.

General Stuart prized Pelham's companionship and insisted

that he live at the cavalry's staff headquarters where he was always on tap for consultation and conversation. Pelham was pleased and flattered at this attention from the distinguished cavalry chief—his only complaint being that General Stuart curtailed his outside social life by keeping him constantly on call.

With the coming of winter "Jeb" called off all reviews and parades. Pelham used this time to instruct his officers and men in artillery tactics and to devise bold new methods of employing the Stuart Horse Artillery. All the while he kept an eye on the welfare of his troops who braved the cold to keep their guns in condition for instant action. Pelham saw that his men drilled enough to keep from getting soft, but he was careful to see that the soldiers from the Deep South who had never before experienced winter weather, were comfortable in their home-made huts at Camp Qui Vive.

In his own spare time Pelham often discussed the future course of the war with Jim Breathed whom he had grown to like and respect immensely. Jim, only a year older than John, had been practicing medicine on the Western frontier when the war broke out. Returning east by train he happened to occupy the seat next to "Jeb" Stuart who like himself was hurrying back to the defense of his native Virginia. At Stuart's urging Breathed joined the cavalry and shortly wound up in the Horse Artillery.

"How long do you think the war will last?" Jim asked John one frosty evening around the blazing campfire.

"I hope it's over in another year, Jim. We have excellent leaders and our troops are in top condition. But even if this reorganized Union army under General McClellan puts up a stiffer fight than the Yanks did at Manassas, I'm sure we'll eventually win. After all, our cause is just."

"I agree," replied Jim, "we simply must have states' rights

rather than submit to domination by the Federal Government."

While snow was still on the ground early in March, orders were received at cavalry headquarters to break camp and cover the withdrawal of General Johnston's army. Reluctantly, Pelham's artillerists assisted General Stuart's troopers burn the enormous storehouses of corn and bacon at Manassas. It would be a long time before the men again smelled the delicious aroma of roasted meat.

As Pelham rode beside "Jeb" Stuart on the way to Richmond, the young commander of the Horse Artillery gravely inquired: "General, why are we burning our supplies and retreating before we are even attacked?"

"Cheer up, my boy," "Jeb" answered in a brotherly manner, "I understand that General McClellan is transporting almost 100,000 bluecoats by boat to the tip of the Peninsula in Virginia where they will attempt to make a sneak march behind our backs and capture Richmond. But we're going to surprise "Little Mac" with a warm reception when he lands."

Pelham was greatly relieved to learn that General Johnston was actually advancing to meet General McClellan rather than retreating from him. He pushed his column with renewed vigor, especially through the streets of Richmond where he was embarrassed by pretty belles who lined the sidewalks to throw him bouquets and kisses.

General Johnston's army, 45,000 strong, reached Yorktown on the lower end of the Peninsula just as warm spring days thawed the snow and turned the dirt roads into mud. Here at Yorktown the veterans of Manassas united with General "Prince John" Magruder's small force of 11,000 graycoats which the blustery Confederate commander had scattered across the narrow neck of the Peninsula to hold off the enemy hordes until General Johnston arrived. "Prince John," who got his nickname because of his striking royal appearance which was set

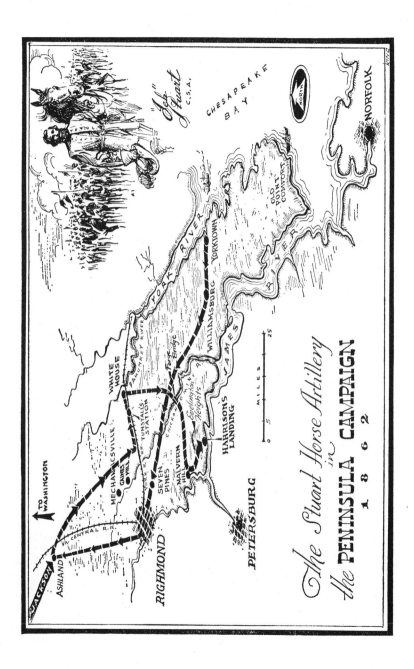

"Jeb" Stuart
C.S.A.

CHESAPEAKE BAY

NORTH

NORFOLK

OLD POINT COMFORT

YORK RIVER

JAMES RIVER

YORKTOWN

WILLIAMSBURG

HARRISON'S LANDING

Malvern Hill

Evelington Heights

WHITE HOUSE

Forge Bridge

TUNSTALL'S STATION

PAMUNKEY RIVER

CHICKAHOMINY

SEVEN PINES

GAINES' MILL

MECHANICSVILLE

TO WASHINGTON

JACKSON

ASHLAND

RICHMOND

VA CENTRAL R.R.

PETERSBURG

MILES
0   5   25

The Stuart Horse Artillery in
the PENINSULA CAMPAIGN
1862

KING

off by gaudily decorated uniforms, had completely bluffed the Yankees into doing nothing by mounting huge logs disguised to look like cannon in the Confederate fortifications.

After eight months of inaction, Pelham was impatient to duel with the enemy artillerists. He had drilled his company in every detail, and now he wanted to put this training into practice. But throughout the rainy month of April General Johnston kept his troops in the fortifications at Yorktown while he tried to convince President Davis that this position should be abandoned. He argued that General McClellan could easily land large bodies of troops at night behind the Confederate lines and then beat the graycoats to Richmond. General Johnston was so worried about this threat that he disregarded President Davis' orders and pulled his troops out of the trenches before dawn on May 4th and headed them back toward Richmond. General Stuart again was the last to leave as the cavalry was ordered to cover the withdrawal against any enemy attack.

Pelham's men cussed as they put their shoulders to the carriages which kept getting stuck in the knee-deep mud. They complained bitterly that "Retreatin' Joe", as they dubbed General Johnston, was scared to let them fight the Yankees. Pelham too was disappointed, but he firmly silenced any criticism of General Johnston in his presence. "You'll get your chance to fight before long," he reassured the gunners, "but it'll be where General Johnston thinks we stand the best chance of beating the Yanks."

Sure enough, about noon the next day a force of General George Stoneman's Federal skirmishers on horseback brushed against General Stuart's rearguard just outside Williamsburg and a fight was on. "Jeb" immediately countered the enemy's move by about-facing his cavalry and calling on Pelham to bring forward the Horse Artillery.

Just as "Jeb" prepared to give the order, "Draw sabers!

Charge!" the enemy delivered a heavy fire on General Stuart's front line troopers. "Jeb" sent a courier to Pelham with orders to silence those pesky bluecoats. But before the message arrived, Pelham had already unlimbered his guns beside Telegraph Road along which the enemy troopers were advancing. Without delay he ordered his guns to fire point-blank into the wave of Federal cavalry which was thundering down the road.

Bluecoated troopers reeled and horses stumbled as they ran into Pelham's barrage. General Stoneman quickly decided to avoid further useless slaughter by ordering a halt to the charge while he brought forward supporting infantry and artillery to silence and capture Pelham's deadly battery. But Captain Pelham held his own against even these odds by timing his fire so that each gun discharged immediately after the one on its left thereby maintaining a continuous fire.

Meanwhile, General Johnston personally led one of General Magruder's brigades into a series of forts or redoubts which had been constructed on the other side of Telegraph to defend Williamsburg in just such an emergency as this. When the gray infantrymen had taken their positions behind the earthworks, General Stuart ordered Captain Pelham to coordinate his artillery fire with the musketry so as to blanket the enemy with a withering cross-fire.

This combined firepower held General McClellan's advance guard at bay until dark. Next day General "Old Pete" Longstreet, a massive, bearded commander with nerves of steel, hurled his division against the heavily reinforced bluecoats and crippled them so severely that they were discouraged from again closely pressing the main Confederate army.

General Stuart, who was always generous in praising his subordinates, gave Captain Pelham full credit for saving the day at Williamsburg. From his "Headquarters in the Saddle" "Jeb" wrote: "I consider the most brilliant feat of the battle to have been a dash of the Stuart Horse Artillery to the front. Coming suddenly under a galling fire only 2,000 yards from the enemy in the woods, they wheeled into action sustaining in the most brilliant manner the fortunes of the day until the infantry could come to their support."

Pelham naturally was pleased at this high praise from his superior. It showed that the high command realized and appreciated the tremendous tactical value of this new mobile artillery unit. The modest Alabamian inwardly resolved to maintain and even enhance this enviable reputation.

However, in the next engagement at Seven Pines, General Stuart's cavalry and Pelham's Horse Artillery were forced to stay on the sidelines while the giant infantry forces slugged it out toe-to-toe in dense woods which immobilized horses. During this one-day battle which ended in a draw, General Johnston was critically wounded in the shoulder and chest. Thereupon President Davis appointed General Robert E. Lee to command of the Army of Northern Virginia. Under this daring and brilliant new leader, Captain Pelham henceforth would be in the forefront of the most aggressive fighting ever seen on this continent.

the wake of battle

Pelham '73 U.S.S. Marblehead

CHAPTER IV

Pounding the Union Army and Navy

Now THAT General McClellan had pushed his mammoth Army of the Potomac to the outskirts of Richmond, he daily sent his chief balloonist, Professor Thaddeus Sobieski Constantine Lowe, aloft in his silken 32,000-cubic foot balloon decorated with the stars and stripes and its name, INTREPID. From his perch in the sky Professor Lowe telegraphed back to headquarters that soldiers and civilians in Richmond were feverishly throwing up a ring of protective earthworks.

However, General Robert E. Lee had no intention of waiting for his cautious opponent to attack. Instead, he planned to take the offensive just as soon as he could ascertain the weak spot in "Little Mac's" long front. On June 10 General Lee summoned General Stuart to his headquarters. After exchanging salutes the commanding General invited the cavalry chief to draw up a chair beside the table on which he had spread a map of Richmond and the Peninsula.

"General Stuart," he began, "I hope to drive the enemy from

Richmond and destroy him as soon as I can obtain certain information about his position and strength."

Then pointing to the blue lines representing the Union army east of Richmond, General Lee continued, "You will notice that the Army of the Potomac is split in two by the Chickahominy River. According to our intelligence reports General Fitz Porter's Fifth Corps is encamped north of the river. I want you to take 1,200 of your cavalry and probe how far General Porter's line extends and how strong it is."

"Jeb" beamed at the prospect of this "expedition," as General Lee called it, which offered an exciting opportunity to scout the enemy's position and obtain the information necessary for mounting a giant Confederate offensive.

"I can start to-morrow night," "Jeb" told General Lee, "and if I find my way clear I'd like to continue riding clear around McClellan's army."

General Lee smiled admiringly at the boldness of his lieutenant's proposal. It was exactly the type of mission he would like to make himself. But he cautioned, "Don't worry about riding around the Union army until you locate the exact position and strength of General Porter's Corps. Then you can decide which course seems advisable."

After leaving this conference General Stuart lost no time issuing orders for his men to cook three-day's rations and saddle up for a long ride. He wanted to take the entire Horse Artillery but realized that General Lee would need some of its guns if the Federals should attack while the cavalry was gone. "Jeb" discussed the matter with Pelham who magnanimously suggested that Jim Breathed accompany the expedition with a twelve-pounder howitzer and a rifled gun. General Stuart agreed to this arrangement, and the next day Pelham longingly waved good-bye to the long column of four horsemen abreast as they rode off on their exciting adventure.

MAJOR GENERAL JAMES E. B. ("JEB") STUART

Lee's daring, jovial chief of cavalry, possessed a magnificent physique which enabled him to campaign for days in the saddle with only a few hours sleep. Friend and foe agreed that he was "the greatest cavalry officer ever foaled in America."

MAJOR HEROS VON BORCKE

This gargantuan Prussian soldier-of-fortune came to America during the Civil War and offered his services to General Stuart who made him an aide. Between battles he entertained the soldiers with his clowning and tall tales.

Fifty-eight hours later General Stuart strode into General Lee's tent to report that he had found General Fitz Porter's Fifth Corps in an exposed position. Finding little opposition, "Jeb" had then proceeded to make a spectacular 150-mile ride around the Army of the Potomac. The commanding General complimented General Stuart on his remarkable feat which at the cost of but one life boosted Southern morale at its low ebb.

When General Lee asked General Stuart for a detailed description of the Union forces north of the Chickahominy River, "Jeb" explained that General Porter had concentrated his 30,000 bluecoats in a small sector north of the river, and that it had not received reinforcements to extend and protect the right flank which lay exposed to the north.

On the basis of this information General Lee issued orders for General Jackson to bring his soldiers from the Shenandoah Valley and join the main army in a combined assault on General Porter's isolated corps. After overwhelming the Federal Fifth Corps, General Lee intended to hurl his Army of Northern Virginia on the rest of General McClellan's army and destroy it.

General Stuart's cavalry and Horse Artillery were instructed to meet General Jackson at Ashland, a village sixteen miles north of Richmond, and screen his march to Mechanicsville. Here General Jackson's divisions were to assail General Porter's exposed right flank while the three powerful divisions of Generals A. P. Hill, "Old Pete" Longstreet and D. H. Hill smashed in the Federal front. However, the march from Ashland to Mechanicsville was delayed, and General Jackson did not arrive at the front until the day after the main Confederate force had attacked and driven the enemy to Gaines' Mill.

Here on the heights overlooking swampland, General Porter drew up his force in three defensive lines supported by heavy artillery. After observing these formidable defenses General

Lee ordered his divisions to attack vigorously all along the line. Throughout the afternoon "Old Pete" Longstreet and A. P. Hill sent their troops charging uphill against a storm of musketry and artillery shells; each time they fell back to re-form and try again.

Meanwhile, General Jackson was delayed in getting his fourteen brigades through the tangled woods and into position to join in the assault. "Stonewall's" difficulties were further aggravated by two pesky Federal batteries which lobbed shells into the advancing gray columns. As General Jackson's own batteries were not yet up, General Stuart offered to send Captain Pelham forward with some of the Horse Artillery. "Stonewall" readily agreed, and Pelham quickly hauled his rifled 12-pounder Blakely and a recently-captured Napoleon gun to a clearing where he opened fire at short range on the enemy's eight guns. The Federal gunners disabled the Blakely with their first salvo, whereupon Pelham shouted: "Blakely gun crew drag your gun back out of range! Men of the Napoleon Detachment, follow me to a new position!"

As the sweating Creoles wheeled the Napoleon into position at the edge of the clearing, Pelham coolly addressed his gunners: "Men, we Alabamians are all that stand between the advancing Yankee batteries and General Jackson's troops. We must rout them so that the Valley infantry can push ahead and join in the main attack."

With this grim message ringing in their ears the singing Creoles went into action chanting the "Marseillaise." For an hour Pelham and his Napoleon Detachment fired so furiously that the two enemy batteries had a difficult time holding their own against the lone Napoleon.

On hearing the brisk fight Captain Pelham was waging, General Jackson inquired how many guns of the Horse Artillery were engaged. "Jeb" Stuart proudly replied, "Captain Pelham now has only one gun in action, but he is fighting like a tiger." When General Jackson's thirty guns finally relieved Pelham late in the afternoon, General Stuart escorted his powder-stained artillerist to "Stonewall" Jackson and said: "General Jackson, here is Captain Pelham who has kept the enemy batteries in check on your front."

"Stonewall" in his faded gray uniform shook Pelham's hand, and said warmly, "Good work, Captain Pelham."

Then as the shadows began to lengthen, General Jackson advanced his infantry and issued orders to "sweep the field with the bayonet!" "Stonewall's" veterans, 18,000 strong, responded on the double and raised the blood-curdling Rebel Yell as they charged the enemy head-on. The long gray lines were not to be denied, and before nightfall they had driven the bluecoats from their entrenchments and chased them across the Chickahominy.

Now that General Lee had the enemy on the run he pondered which way the bluecoats would retreat. The Union supply base was located at White House on the Pamunkey River, but General McClellan seemed to be heading in the opposite direction toward the James River. In this dilemma General Lee sent for "Jeb" Stuart whom he told: "General Stuart, I want you to take your cavalry and destroy General McClellan's lines of communication to his rich supplies at White House."

Early the next morning the cavalry and Horse Artillery galloped away on their mission. En route they cut telegraph wires, seized wagon trains, brushed aside pickets and tore up the railroad tracks of the York River Railroad that ran from Richmond to White House.

When the gray column reached Tunstall's Station, General Stuart noticed a squadron of enemy cavalry supported by artillery drawn up on a high muddy bank across the river known as Black Creek. With the bridge burned even "Jeb" Stuart did not dare risk fording the river under heavy enemy fire. Therefore, he summoned Pelham and explained the situation. "Captain", he concluded, "I want you to disperse the enemy with your cannon."

Within a few minutes Pelham's men had unlimbered two howitzers in a concealed position from which a salvo sent the Yankee troopers scurrying for cover. Then seeing some suspicious movements in the underbrush bordering the opposite bank of the river, Pelham shouted the order: "Change to canister and fire at the bank!" Sure enough, the first barrage flushed a company of bluecoats out of the green bushy camouflage underneath which they had lain in ambush for the cavalry and Horse Artillery.

In their haste to flee to safety the Federals abandoned two slightly used rifled guns which General Stuart turned over to Pelham. Next morning General Stuart led his column toward distant clouds of black smoke rising above the depot at White House. The enemy obviously was burning his enormous stores to prevent them from falling into Confederate hands.

Finding that the enemy had a powerful gunboat anchored in the river plus a two-to-one superiority in numbers, General Stuart smartly resorted to a ruse to oust the gunboat and bluecoats from White House. He sent for Pelham and said: "Captain, our friends in the neighborhood inform me that there are 5,000 Yankees defending this town. We don't have enough troops to charge them head-on, but we can out-maneuver them. I plan to dismount seventy-five sharpshooters and station them forty paces apart on the meadow bordering the river where they can pepper the crew of the gunboat which I understand is the U.S.S. Marblehead. The enemy will mistake these men for infantry and figure that we would not dare attack unless we had a strong force in reserve. Meanwhile, you are to take a howitzer and lob shells at the gunboat from long range. Take position where the gunboat cannot bring its 11-inch naval guns to bear on you. Also change position often so that the enemy will think we are using a number of cannon."

While Pelham hauled his cannon into position, "Jeb's" sharp-shooters opened fire with their carbines on the bluecoats lining the deck of the Marblehead. The New York soldiers aboard immediately answered the challenge with a salvo from the naval guns. Then a company of soldiers was lowered into two boats and rowed to the bank from which the Confederates were firing steadily.

On wading ashore the Yankees formed in line and engaged Stuart's marksmen in a brisk skirmish. At this juncture Pelham opened fire from the woods with his howitzer. Employing his customary skill Pelham sighted the target so accurately that the spherical case shells burst directly over the decks of the Marblehead, spreading consternation among the men and officers who could not locate and reply to the gun which was harassing them.

In accordance with General Stuart's orders, Pelham kept changing position after firing a few rounds. His fire was so intense and accurate that the commander of the Marblehead soon decided not to risk having his ship sunk at anchor. He had his bugler blow the retreat, whereupon the landing party withdrew to the gunboat which lifted anchor and steamed away.

But Pelham was not one to let this moving target run away unchallenged. He limbered up the howitzer and galloped along the shore parallel to the boat. At intervals he ordered his men to stop, fire a few shells, and then dash ahead and "salute" the gunboat again. This continued until the Marblehead finally scurried out of range.

His mission accomplished, Pelham led his crew to the burning town, now deserted by the enemy infantry who had fled on Stuart's approach. When he reported to General Stuart, the cavalry chief warmly clasped Pelham's hand and said: "Well done, Captain, you certainly handled the Union Navy as roughly as you do the Army of the Potomac."

Pelham smiled at the compliment, and replied: "Thanks, General. At least I don't think we'll be bothered by the Marblehead for a while."

Turning toward the smoking ruins of the town, "Jeb" said, "Pelham my boy, take your crew and help yourselves to the bountiful provisions our Yankee friends were unable to destroy in their hurry to escape."

Pelham's cannoneers needed no second invitation to join Stuart's troopers in tackling the fancy luxuries intended for General McClellan's army. Hungry Southern lads who had lived the past few days on salt meat and crackers now feasted on tropical fruits, lemonade, preserved eggs, meat, fish, French rolls, candy, Havana cigars and assorted liquors. When some of the troopers began to get tipsy from sampling the whiskey, Colonel "Rooney" Lee, General Lee's second son, started a rumor that the enemy had poisoned the liquor to get even with the Confederates. The story spread swiftly causing many red-faced celebrators to throw away their flasks and hold their stomachs in imagined agony. Colonel Lee's ruse successfully halted further drinking.

Pelham and Jim Breathed feasted on pickled oysters and fruit under the shade of a tree beside the river. After finishing a juicy pear, Jim commented, "Captain, if McClellan's troops eat like this every day it's no wonder they run away rather than fight and get killed."

"Yes," said John, smiling, "the Union army retreats on a full stomach while we advance on empty one. Maybe we fight better than they do in order to capture a square meal like this one."

While these two artillerists discussed the effect of food on a soldier's morale, General Stuart rode up and joined them. "Gentlemen," he said, "I find that the enemy has left behind several locomotives undamaged. We can't take them with us, but they may later be useful to our government. Therefore, I want you to disable them with your guns without destroying the costly parts."

Pelham and Breathed quickly finished their meal and rode to the rail yard where the locomotives were lined up back of each other. After sizing up the situation, John said: "Jim, what do you think of firing a shell through the middle of each boiler?"

"That should do the job perfectly," Breathed replied. "It will break some tubes and puncture the sides making the locomotives useless to the enemy, but our shops in Richmond can repair them easily."

Pelham then ordered up a rifled gun which he placed about fifty yards from each locomotive and shot a neat hole through the boiler.

Victory-happy Confederates celebrated the rest of this eventful Sabbath exchanging their frayed equipment and clothing for brand-new items from abandoned sutlers' stores which supplied the Union army. Late in the afternoon Pelham and Breathed strolled down to the river to watch flames devour several large barges laden with supplies which the enemy had set afire before fleeing.

General Stuart's cavalry and Horse Artillery now had been separated from General Lee's army for two days. "Jeb" decided that having cut General McClellan's line of communications to his supply base at White House, it was time for the raiders to rejoin the main army. Accordingly, after reveille the next morning the troopers and Horse Artillery headed toward the winding Chickahominy River whose banks were overgrown with thick summer foliage.

On reaching the wooded hills above Forge Bridge, General

Stuart espied a force of enemy infantry, cavalry and artillery drawn up on the opposite bank. "Jeb" sent a note by courier to Pelham ordering him to bring forward two howitzers and engage the Union battery.

"Make way for the Horse Artillery," Pelham shouted, and the cavalry column opened ranks to permit cannons and caissons to jounce to the front. With his excellent eye for terrain, Pelham instantly selected a position about 400 yards from the bridge. Here his men unlimbered the fieldpieces which Pelham then sighted.

At the command, "Ready! Fire!" the howitzers opened an arching fire on the enemy guns which made a feeble answer and then limbered up and galloped to the rear. Now that the enemy's guns were silenced, "Jeb" Stuart led his troopers across the bridge in hot pursuit. Meantime, Pelham advanced his cannon to the bridge where they maintained a demoralizing fire on the retreating Yankees.

At the close of this busy, hot day Pelham and his boys treated themselves to luscious cherries in a grove near Forge Bridge. That evening, however, their sleep was disturbed by the distant booming of heavy artillery. Eager to join the fray, General Stuart roused his command before daybreak and galloped across the Peninsula toward the sound of battle. After riding forty-two miles, Stuart and Pelham joined General Jackson at Malvern Hill just as darkness ended the savage battle.

Around the campfire that night Pelham learned that General Lee had caught up with and attacked General McClellan's army as it retreated across the Peninsula to the James River. But here at Malvern Hill "Little Mac" had massed 350 heavy guns which slaughtered 5,000 Confederates as they bravely charged up the mile and a half slope.

Now that he had warded off General Lee's rearguard attack,

General McClellan appeared to be heading safely toward his new base on the James. However, General Stuart reasoned that the enemy was badly demoralized after a week of beatings and retreats. With this in mind he summoned Pelham and outlined a bold plan he had in mind.

"Captain," he said excitedly, "I want you to take your most serviceable howitzer together with one of my cavalry squadrons and scout the enemy's position. Discover whether their camps are guarded and check the lay of the land to determine whether we can possibly bottle them up and clobber their troops with artillery. I don't need to tell you to go like lightning, but be careful to avoid engaging a large enemy force."

After a salute and warm handshake Pelham darted into the darkness to prepare for his mission. He was gratified that his chief entrusted him with such an important assignment which might obtain the information necessary for General Lee to crush the enemy and perhaps end the war.

On returning to his unit Pelham delegated Jim Breathed to take command of the Horse Artillery during his absence. Then he hand-picked a group to accompany him. Lieutenant Bill McGregor, a fellow Alabamian, would be second in command. The crew was composed largely of Creoles from the Napoleon Detachment. Fifteen-year-old Jean smiled with joy as Pelham read his name among those who were to accompany him.

Deftly the young men filled the caisson and limber. When curious soldiers from other units gathered around the howitzer to inquire what movement was afoot, Pelham smilingly replied with a wink, "We're going to call on General McClellan."

Within a few minutes preparations were complete, whereupon Pelham and McGregor mounted their sorrels and led the small party into the night. Fortunately, battle smoke from the afternoon's artillery engagement darkened the sky making it difficult for the enemy to identify the gray-uniformed unit.

Stealthily the group followed little-used paths and dirt roads parallel to the route taken by the retreating bluecoats.

Before long a heavy rain fell. To the right Pelham heard soldiers grunt and swear as they pushed ambulance wagons which kept getting stuck in the mud. He could not help but sympathize with the maimed and wounded inside the ambulance wagons who cried out in shrieks of pain as the vehicles jolted along the bumpy country roads.

Near Rawling's Mill Pond Pelham observed the Federal column veer to the right toward the spacious plantations bordering the James River at Harrison's Landing. After carefully feeling his way to make certain that General McClellan's entire army was heading toward the river, Pelham led his men to a rise known as Evelington Heights. From this elevation waving wheatfields sloped down gradually for about a mile to the river where a fleet of gunboats lay silhouetted against the sky. Onto this plain bordered by a stream known as Herring Creek, "Little Mac" was herding his divisions and artillery for a last ditch stand. Pelham noted that in his haste to pitch tents and start campfires with damp wood the enemy had neglected to post pickets to guard the camp. Turning to Bill McGregor, Pelham said: "If General McClellan will only remain like this until we can rush guns and troops to these heights we can annihilate the Army of the Potomac."

"Yes," replied McGregor, "with enough reinforcements we could drive the Yankees into the river."

Pelham realized, however, that a commander as able and cautious as General McClellan would soon discover this exposed condition and take steps to correct it. Therefore, Pelham lost no time in carefully examining the ground around Evelington Heights so that he could report to General Stuart the best position for a surprise attack. This done, he quietly and quickly led his squad back along the muddy trails to cavalry headquarters.

It was not quite dawn when "Jeb" Stuart's orderly roused him with the news that Captain Pelham had returned from his mission. The cavalry leader, who had been dozing on a cot in his tent with his clothes on, instantly rose and invited Pelham to come in out of the rain. As the two comrades sat on campstools, Pelham described his adventure and asked for a map of the area.

Running his finger along the lines representing the roads from Malvern Hill to Harrison's Landing (a distance not quite ten miles), Pelham pointed to Evelington Heights and said fervidly: "General McClellan has concentrated his army on the plain below this ridge. When we left him a few hours ago the heights commanding his position were unoccupied even by sentinels. If we hurry with sufficient forces I think we can crush the whole Yankee army."

At this statement General Stuart rose from his chair, his eyes burning with anticipation. As "Jeb" buckled on his handsome curved cavalry sword and thoughtfully ran the plume of his hat through his powerful fingers, Pelham surmised what was coming. "Let's go," Stuart declared grimly.

By eight o'clock Pelham had guided General Stuart and his cavalry regiments to Evelington Heights which was now occupied by a Federal cavalry squadron drawn up in a long line with banners flying. Without hesitation "Jeb" rose in his stirrups, turned to his leading regiment, and shouted: "Form fours! Draw sabers! Charge!"

Before the startled enemy commander could rally his troopers to meet Stuart's charge the graycoats were upon them— lashing out furiously with gleaming sabers. Unable to withstand this fierce onslaught, the Yankees broke ranks and fled toward the river.

Confederate cavalry now held the ridge from which Stuart's horsemen and Pelham's guns commanded a sweeping view of the sprawling Union army which was then engaged in preparing breakfast. Knowing that "Stonewall" Jackson and "Old Pete" Longstreet were following him with infantry, "Jeb" simply couldn't resist the temptation to throw a scare into the Federal camp. Laying a hand on Pelham's shoulder, he said, "Captain, I want you to take a howitzer to a concealed position and let 'em have it."

Pelham knew just the spot from which to launch such a surprise barrage. The previous night, while reconnoitering to the left along Herring Creek, he had come upon quaint, spired Westover Church. In the open lot behind this edifice the crew quickly unlimbered the howitzer and began hurling 12-pound shells among the startled enemy.

The first shells whistled over the plain to strike the boats, on one of which General McClellan had established his headquarters. Pelham then shortened the range to spread consternation among the troops. As wagons overturned, tents toppled, and horses reared, the enemy infantry grabbed muskets from stands of stacked arms and formed to repel this surprise attack.

General Stuart meanwhile had spread his sharpshooters along the ridge to meet the enemy's advance. And Pelham's cannon began dueling with an entire Union battery. Pelham fired his howitzer rapidly and changed position often to give the impression that a number of fieldpieces were wreaking all the havoc.

When the 11-inch guns on the gunboats opened on Pelham, General Stuart retaliated by bringing up a Congrieve rocket battery which fired huge rockets from a modified gun carriage. Zooming through the air in a zig-zag course the missiles exploded in the enemy camp spreading "liquid damnation," as the cheering graycoats called it. Tents caught fire and mules stampeded as the liquid contents sprayed a wide area.

However, the Federals realized that they were fighting with their backs to the river and that defeat meant final surrender. Therefore, General McClellan organized a strong force to drive the Confederates from Evelington Heights. Stuart and Pelham bravely stood their ground against vastly superior numbers and firepower for five hours, expecting infantry support to arrive at any moment and turn the tide. But when a courier reported to General Stuart in mid-afternoon that General Longstreet had taken the wrong road and gotten lost, "Jeb" realized it would be suicide to try to hold out longer alone. He summoned his bugler and ordered him to sound the retreat.

Reluctantly, Pelham helped limber his smoking howitzer—now down to two rounds of ammunition—and haul it to a safe position two miles away. Here "Stonewall" Jackson's and "Old Pete" Longstreet's divisions arrived the next morning ready to attack. However, General McClellan by now had fortified Evelington Heights so strongly with infantry and artillery that General Lee decided it would be too costly to launch an offensive with his battle-weary army.

Nevertheless, Stuart and Pelham continued to harass the enemy. During the night "Jeb" took a cavalry regiment and escorted Pelham with six of his guns to a concealed position on the bank of the James River below Harrison's Landing. Pelham ordered his men to load the guns so as to be ready to fire at an instant's notice.

Shortly a flotilla of five Federal troop transports hove into view. Deck lanterns revealed crowds of Union soldiers who were on their way to reinforce the Army of the Potomac. When the boats skirted the shore within a range of 100 yards Pelham shouted the order, "Fire!" Six cannon simultaneously hurtled shells through the air and onto the decks where they exploded, sinking one transport and inflicting heavy damage on the other. Pelham continued to shower destruction on the crippled boats until several gunboats rushed to their aid.

Back at camp Captain Pelham shared General Lee's disappointment that the Army of Northern Virginia had not destroyed General McClellan's Army of the Potomac. On the credit side, however, Pelham cheered his men by reassuring them that they had covered themselves with glory in the grueling Seven Days Battles during which the indomitable graycoats hurled the enemy back from the gates of Richmond.

Surprise attack

CHAPTER V

"Always in the Right Place at the Right Time"

WHILE General McClellan's battered Union army bathed its wounds in the James River, General Robert E. Lee led his army back to the camps around Richmond for a well-earned rest. Much to his surprise and embarrassment, Pelham now discovered that he was regarded as a hero throughout the army.

Around the evening campfires, sunburned veterans of the Seven Days Battles never tired of relating Captain Pelham's feats: how with a single Napoleon he checked the advance of eight enemy guns at Gaines' Mill; how he routed the Yankees lying in ambush at Black Creek; how with a lone howitzer he out-duelled the 11-inch guns on the U.S.S. Marblehead and sent the gunboat scurrying down the Pamunkey; how he blasted the bluecoats out of "Jeb" Stuart's path at Forge Bridge; how with only one howitzer he boldly fired into the entire Federal army at Harrison's Landing; and, finally, how he scrappily attacked a flotilla of enemy transports, actually sinking one.

General Stuart proudly shared the general admiration for his blond young commander of the Stuart Horse Artillery. In his report to General Lee, the cavalry chief wrote:

"Captain John Pelham, of the Horse Artillery, displayed such signal ability as an artillerist, such heroic example and devotion in danger, and indomitable energy under difficulties in the movement of his battery, that, reluctant as I am at the chance of losing such a valuable limb from the brigade, I feel bound to ask for his promotion, with the remark that in either cavalry or artillery no field grade is too high for his merit and capacity."

Captain Pelham naturally appreciated the compliments paid him, but they made him uncomfortable. When others mentioned his deeds, he blushed and modestly replied that he was simply fortunate to have abler gunners than the Yankees. When promotions were announced later in the summer, General Stuart called Pelham to his tent and with a warm smile said: "Pelham, my boy, accept my sincere congratulations. General Lee wants me to tell you that, in his opinion, your masterly handling of the Horse Artillery contributed greatly to our recent successes. In recognition of your outstanding services you are to be promoted to the rank of Major in the Confederate States Army."

With Major Pelham's new rank came a three-fold increase in responsibilities. To his own battery were added Captain Robert P. Chew's Virginia battery and Captain Jim Hart's South Carolina battery. With his characteristic zeal and efficiency, Pelham set about to weld the three batteries into a smoothly-running unit.

During the rest of July and most of August General Stuart's command, now 3,000 strong, drilled on the flatlands around Hanover Court House north of Richmond. From time to time "Jeb" staged full-dress cavalry reviews which were attended by his lovely wife, Flora, and many admiring young belles in the area who drove up in horse-drawn carriages.

After the colorful parades, General Stuart invited the ladies to visit his camp where he served them milk and ginger cookies.

In introducing his staff, the cavalry chief enjoyed embarrassing Pelham by presenting him to the flirtatious young ladies as "my eligible artillerist." Thereupon the blond Major's face reddened as he graciously acknowledged the introduction and stammeringly tried to make conversation. But before long he overcame his extreme shyness and gained the reputation of being "as grand a flirt as ever lived."

Each evening after supper General Stuart assembled his staff around the campfire at his headquarters. Here the officers swapped yarns, chatted about their loved ones back home, and sang their favorite song, "If You Want To Have Fun, Jine the Cavalry," accompanied by Sam Sweeney on his banjo.

Major Pelham especially enjoyed listening to Major Heros von Borcke describe his experiences in gutteral English. Von Borcke was a giant Prussian who weighed 250 pounds and towered six-feet-four inches in height. He was so bulky around the middle that he couldn't tie his shoes. The Major had been a lieutenant in the Cuirassiers of the Guard in Berlin. This regiment was officered by men of high station, but when von Borcke's father refused to support his son's wild extravagances, the young giant pulled up stakes and came to America where he became a member of General Stuart's staff. Blessed with a keen sense of humor, this soldier-of-fortune entertained the group around the campfire for hours with tales of the Prussian army and his escapades in slipping through the Northern blockade to join the Confederacy.

Early in August General Stuart's scouts reported that 8,000 enemy troops had left Fredericksburg and were heading southward toward the Virginia Central Railroad over which the Confederacy shipped provisions from the rich Shenandoah Valley to Richmond. To prevent the destruction of this vital supply artery, "Jeb" galloped northward with four cavalry regiments and the Stuart Horse Artillery.

Near Massaponax Church the cavalry chief espied in the distance a long column of infantry followed by a chain of supply wagons. Quickly he pulled his troopers out of sight to the side of the road, while Pelham divided his guns and posted them behind tall bushes on each flank of the approaching bluecoats. After the enemy foot-soldiers passed the concealed Confederates, General Stuart sent one regiment to capture the wagon train. Then as the bugler sounded the charge, "Jeb" led the other three regiments in a furious assault against the rear of the astonished infantry. Simultaneously, Pelham raced across the fields on both sides of the enemy column and opened fire. Within a few minutes the Federals, confused by attacks from all sides except the front, broke ranks and scattered in all directions.

In this brief but decisive action, General Stuart captured two-hundred prisoners and a number of well-provisioned wagons which he presented to General Lee. That evening small parties of bluecoats straggled back to Fredericksburg, discouraged by Stuart's sabers and Pelham's guns from further demonstrations against the Virginia Central Railroad.

In August, President Lincoln sent a fresh Federal army to open a new front against General Lee in central Virginia. The commander of this force, known as the Army of Virginia, was General John B. Pope, who boasted that he had just come from the West where he always "saw the backs of our enemies."

To meet this threat, General Jackson hurried northward with about 18,000 of his "foot cavalry." At Cedar Mountain, "Stonewall" met the enemy's advance guard and hurled it back on General Pope's main force in Culpeper. This action gave General Lee time to rush "Old Pete" Longstreet's divisions to Gordonsville where the Army of Northern Virginia was reunited and ready for General Pope.

By mid-August General Lee and General Pope faced each

other across the Rappahannock River above its junction with the Rapidan. General Lee was eager to take the offensive, but he realized that a direct assault across the river would be suicidal. Thereupon, he summoned Generals Jackson, Longstreet and Stuart to a council of war at which he presented a bold plan to strike at the enemy.

This audacious strategy involved nothing less than the division of the Army of Northern Virginia into two parts. General Lee was to remain on the Rappahannock with "Old Pete's" thirteen brigades to pin down Pope's army, while "Stonewall" swept wide around the enemy's flank and struck the Union supply lines far behind the front. The cavalry and Horse Artillery would screen General Jackson's march from prying enemy eyes. All commanders agreed enthusiastically to General Lee's strategy.

During the night of August 25, General Jackson roused his men and quick-stepped the gray column up the river and around Pope's flank. Major Pelham's horse-drawn guns and caissons spread out along the right of "Stonewall's" infantry where they could hold off any enemy attack until the infantry could change front and counterattack.

When the enemy failed to appear, "Stonewall's" veterans began slipping out of line to snatch green apples and unripe corn which they devoured to satisfy their empty stomachs. Pelham, astride his sorrel, watched admiringly as General Jackson rode back and forth along the column discouraging straggling and hurrying his troops forward with the command: "Close up, men, close up; push on, push on!"

Pelham commented to "Jeb" Stuart that General Jackson rested his men for ten minutes every hour.

"Yes," replied "Jeb", "General Jackson has found that his troops can cover more ground and remain in fighting condition at all times if they have rest periods at frequent intervals."

By the end of the first day Jackson's striking force had crossed the Rappahannock and marched through Orlean to Salem—a distance of twenty-five miles. Next morning the troops passed through Thoroughfare Gap—a pass in the Bull Run Mountains which the Federals had left unguarded. At Haymarket General Stuart seized a dozen enemy horsemen to prevent them from spreading the news that 20,000 graycoats were threatening General Pope's rear.

At Gainesville the column turned right toward Bristoe Station, four miles distant. Friendly residents along the way told the footsore Confederates that the enemy had posted only a small force to guard the Bristoe railroad bridge over which the Orange and Alexandria Railroad transported troops and supplies to General Pope.

Stimulated by the prospect of wrecking Pope's supply line, the gray-clad troops gained their second wind and hurried forward. Half a mile from Bristoe Station, General Jackson halted the head of his column to allow the rear brigades to close up. Meanwhile, Stuart and Pelham spread the cavalry and Horse Artillery in front of the foot-soldiers to conceal the large number of General Jackson's infantry from view of the bluecoats guarding the station. While the graycoats were thus busily engaged, two short freight trains managed to whizz through safely and spread the alarm in Washington.

Pelham, annoyed that these trains had passed by unscathed, impatiently asked his superior: "General Stuart, I would like to wheel my six guns into position on the knoll above the station. A direct cannon hit on the engine boiler would stop the next train. Then General Jackson's troops and your troopers could overwhelm the Yankees as they scramble out of the cars."

"No," replied "Jeb" smiling at his artillerist's spirit, "save your shells for General Pope's main army. We'll wreck the trains by derailing them. Listen, here comes one now!"

Through the darkness to the south came the shriek of an engine whistle, whereupon "Stonewall's" advance regiment rushed forward and scattered the Union guards. Other infantry lined up alongside the tracks by the derailing switch to fire at the crew in the engine of the approaching train. Unaware of any danger, the engineer struck the open switch at full steam. To the joy of the waiting graycoats the engine jumped the tracks, lunged wildly over the open ground and jack-knifed over an embankment. Great was the disappointment, however, when no bluecoats emerged from the empty cars.

Shortly, another empty troop-train en route to Washington from General Pope's army ploughed into the wreckage of the first train and twenty more cars overturned. When the engineer of still another train spied the heap of splintered boxcars on the tracks ahead, he speedily reversed his engine and carried the information back to General Pope.

Having wrecked two troop trains, "Stonewall's" men next completed the job of disrupting the enemy's supply line by burning the nearby railroad bridge across Broad Run. But instead of retreating along the route he had come, General Jackson headed his exuberant troops northward toward Manassas Junction where they reaped a bountiful reward in the form of trainloads of General Pope's fabulous supplies.

Here only a year ago Pelham had helped General Jackson check General McDowell's advance until reinforcements arrived for the decisive counterattack. Now the little hamlet was lonesome save for two Federal batteries which had been ordered to guard the trains. General Jackson's advance guard consisting of troops from Georgia and North Carolina let the enemy fire a salvo after which they rushed forward and captured the crews before they could reload.

Then, as if a whistle had blown, the Confederate soldiers and troopers broke ranks and took possession of the hundred freight

Jackson's raid at Manassas

cars and sutlers' stores which bulged with luxuries that Pelham and his men had not enjoyed since the raid on White House early in the summer. With his immense sword, Major von Borcke—vigorously puffing on a "captured" Yankee cigar—pried open crates and barrels filled with canned goods, cheeses, fruit, pickled oysters, rock candy, shoes, saddles, underwear, coats and mattresses.

While soldiers stuffed their stomachs and tried on new clothes, an enemy brigade that had been notified of General Jackson's presence by one of the fleeing trains, approached from the direction of Bull Run. "Stonewall" rode ahead and demanded that they surrender. When the bluecoats answered by grazing Jackson's hat with a Minié ball, the enraged graycoats charged and drove the enemy back across Bull Run. Pelham supported the infantry by bringing up his guns and hurling shells among the retreating Federals who scampered in all directions to avoid being hit.

After capturing 300 prisoners and dispersing the enemy, the exuberant Confederates returned to continue helping themselves to Pope's vast stores which included three brand-new rifled guns that Pelham took for the Horse Artillery. What the men couldn't eat or wear they loaded in their knapsacks. General Jackson's foot soldiers claimed that the cavalry and Horse Artillery had an unfair advantage in being able to carry additional sacks of booty on their horses and caissons. Pelham jokingly told them: "you know the saying—'If you want to have fun, jine the cavalry!' "

That night General Jackson ordered some of his men to set fire to the remaining supplies so as to cripple General Pope. Meanwhile, the cavalry and rest of the infantry marched away by the light of the raging flames toward Groveton on the Warrenton Turnpike. Pelham parked his battery behind the in-

fantry which went into camp along the wooded ridge parallel
to the turnpike.

At cavalry headquarters that night the young officers joked
about the "smoked" bacon they had left at Manassas for General Pope's army.

"Billy Yank can hold a tremendous fire sale of the charred
stuff we just left behind," laughed Pelham.

"Yes," added Jim Breathed, "he'll really be 'burned up' at
us when he sees that mountain of ashes."

Turning to "Jeb" Stuart, Pelham inquired seriously, "General, what do you think General Pope will do when he learns
that we have cut his communications and destroyed a major supply base?"

After a moment's reflection, General Stuart replied:

"He's probably storming back to crush us before General Lee
can move to join us with General Longstreet's divisions . . . if
Pope could crush us he'd then move to Thoroughfare Gap and
strike the other half of our army. But my scouts inform me that
General Longstreet is hurrying and should unite with us shortly.
Then we'll give Pope the surprise of his life!"

Next morning Pelham and Stuart rose early to scan the western horizon for clouds of dust which would signal the approach
of General Longstreet's troops. Through his field-glasses, General Stuart saw dust billowing up from Thoroughfare Gap.
"They're coming through the Gap," he said jubilantly. "Yes,"
rejoined Pelham, "but if my hearing is correct, I hear musketry
there which would indicate the enemy is disputing General
Longstreet's advance." "Don't worry," "Jeb" replied confidently, "the bluecoats won't detain "Old Pete" very long."

Meantime, General Jackson had come into possession of intercepted enemy dispatches which indicated that General Pope's
army was thundering toward the isolated Confederate force
at Groveton. This was exactly what "Stonewall" wanted his

adversary to do, and he calmly set about preparing a "warm reception." He formed his brigades just inside the woods along the ridge parallel to the turnpike. During the hot summer afternoon the waiting graycoats relaxed in the shade and quenched their thirst with cold buttermilk furnished by friendly farmers in the neighborhood.

Shortly before sunset the strains of a regimental band drifted up the turnpike from the direction of Gainesville. Instantly the graycoats were on their feet, their eyes focussed on the column of bluecoats marching along the road. While the soldiers in the woods checked their muskets and cartridge cases, they were startled to see General Jackson suddenly emerge from the woods and ride out alone to get a close look at the long line of enemy troops.

"Why does General Jackson take a chance of being shot by enemy skirmishers at such close range?" Jim Breathed anxiously asked Pelham.

"He probably wants to find out how far the Yankee column extends," replied Pelham with obvious admiration for "Stonewall's" complete disregard of danger.

When he was satisfied that this was only one division of Pope's army, "Stonewall" rode slowly back to the woods determined to crush the unsuspecting foe. Riding up to his officers, he said quietly, "Bring up your men." As the infantry formed ranks for the attack, Pelham galloped away to bring up the Horse Artillery.

At the command, "Forward!" "Guide center, march!" the famous "Stonewall" Brigade and three batteries rushed out of the woods and down the sloping plain to assail the startled bluecoats. Stopping about a hundred yards from the turnpike, "Stonewall's" veterans opened at point-blank range on the Yankees who were now changing front to receive the charge.

However, General Jackson quickly realized that he had

greatly underestimated the fighting prowess of these Federal troops. His valiant "Stonewall" Brigade had taken on the stubborn Iron Brigade composed of Wisconsin farmers who were conspicuous in their tall, bell-crowned black hats which added to their naturally rugged appearance. The toughest brigades in each army were now locked in a fierce struggle.

The Iron Brigade returned volley with volley while Yankee artillerists brought up their superior rifled guns on the flanks to duel General Jackson's batteries. At this juncture Pelham arrived at the front with two trusty Blakelys. He reported to General Jackson who ordered an aide to guide him into position. As Pelham's crews unlimbered the guns, enemy infantry greeted them with a volley. Undaunted, Pelham coolly directed the placement of his cannon, after which he commanded: "Double-shot both guns with canister!"

While the men hastened to obey, Pelham sat calmly on his horse without moving a muscle. He merely focussed his piercing blue eyes on the tall Yankee silhouettes barely visible in the growing darkness. When his gunners yelled, "Ready, Major," Pelham rose in his stirrups and shouted, "Fire!"

For over an hour the battle raged along the mile-long front with neither side yielding. As men fell others took their places and closed ranks. At one time the bluecoats advanced to within fifty yards of Pelham's fieldpieces, whereupon General Jackson sent word for Pelham to pull his guns back. However, the pole on the right gun had been shattered by an enemy shell making the cannon difficult to move. Hence Pelham remained where he was and directed its fire while the other Blakely kept shifting position to avoid taking a direct hit.

As though by mutual agreement both sides ceased firing at nine o'clock. Neither side had yielded an inch, but both had lost heavily. The "Stonewall" Brigade alone lost a third of its roster together with five officers, and the Iron Brigade

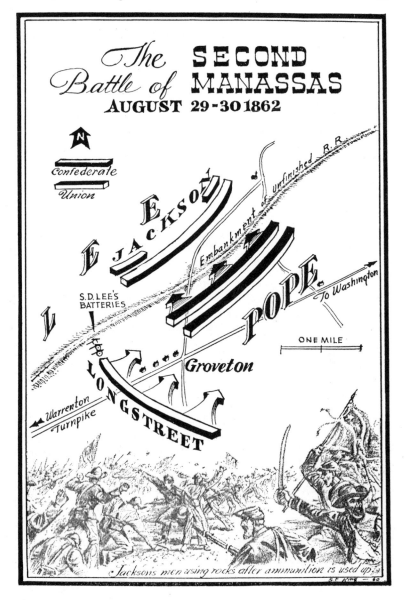

The **SECOND MANASSAS**
The Battle of
AUGUST 29-30 1862

N

Confederate
Union

L E E
JACKSON
Embankment of unfinished R.R.
POPE
To Washington
S.D. LEE'S
BATTERIES
ONE MILE
Groveton
Warrenton
Turnpike
LONGSTREET

Jackson's men using rocks after ammunition is used up.

S.F. KING — 60

suffered 750 casualties out of 2,000 who had answered the roll that morning. Burying parties found the dead lying in parallel lines where they had fallen without breaking ranks.

Late that night the surviving enemy troops resumed their march northward, while General Jackson posted his veterans behind a railroad embankment about a mile opposite the position he had occupied the previous summer at the Battle of First Manassas.

Beneath a starry August sky exhausted Confederates slept so soundly on their arms that they did not hear the distant shouts of General Pope's divisions which were uniting for the kill. In his tent, General Jackson composed his report of the day's battle at Groveton. Although "Stonewall" was usually sparing in his praise, he could not restrain himself from expressing his appreciation of Pelham's superb handling of the Horse Artillery. He wrote: "Owing to the difficulty of getting through the woods, I did not have as much of that arm as I desired at the opening of the engagement; but this want was met by Major Pelham with the Stuart Horse Artillery, who dashed forward on my right and opened upon the enemy at a moment when his services were much needed." To General Jackson's praise, "Jeb" Stuart added: "Pelham is always in the right place at the right time."

General Pope was now certain he had "Stonewall" in a trap where he could destroy him before General Lee could reunite his divided army. During the night the confident Federal commander issued orders for 25,000 bluecoats to attack Jackson's rear while another 25,000 assailed his front.

However, General Pope's blustery activities failed to disturb "Stonewall", who carefully inspected his two-mile front along the railroad cut. Early in the morning he dispatched General Stuart to guide "Old Pete" Longstreet's troops to the position they were to occupy on Jackson's right.

Before departing, "Jeb" directed Pelham to report to General Jackson for orders. Espying "Stonewall" in his frayed uniform, his dingy kepi cap drawn down over his forehead, Pelham galloped up and saluted: "Major Pelham desires to report to General Jackson for orders," he said.

"Come, Major," Jackson replied absently, "and ride with me over the field."

As the two officers galloped along the front from right to left they passed the divisions of Starke, Lawton and A.P. Hill. General Jackson took pains to show Pelham exactly where he had posted the forty guns of his own command so as to sweep the plains beyond which the bluecoats were massing for an attack. Drawing rein behind General Hill's "Light Division," "Stonewall" said to Pelham: "Major, we must stand on the defensive today until General Longstreet arrives. When the enemy strikes I want you to rush the Horse Artillery to the threatened sector and drive him back. I am giving you discretionary orders to employ your guns where and when you deem best."

"Yes, General," replied Pelham, flushing with pride at the unusual compliment the great "Stonewall" had just paid him by personally guiding the young artillerist over the battlefield and then granting him complete freedom to use his own judgment in deploying the Horse Artillery.

Pelham decided for the time being to park his guns in a field behind the extreme left wing of General Hill's division. Just as the crews were about to unlimber the cannons, Pelham heard the crackle of musketry in the woods to his left. Turning toward the sound of firing he saw that a force of enemy cavalry had slipped around General Hill's flank and was now crashing out of the timbers toward the Confederate supply train containing food and ammunition. Seeing that only a handful of wagon drivers stood in the way of the attackers, Pelham shouted: "Into battery! Fire!"

In a flash the Napoleon Detachment was spewing grape and canister into the Federal troopers who drew their sabers and headed straight for the wagons, guns, and cannoneers. Horses stumbled, hurling their riders sprawling on the ground; other bluecoats stopped bullets and tumbled out of their saddle; but some succeeded in breaking through to the guns and wagons. In desperate hand-to-hand fighting the Creoles fought off the enemy, who overturned some of the canvas-covered wagons. During this scuffle little Jean swung his hot sponger at the mounted Yankees, several of whom he gleefully dismounted.

Pelham earnestly rallied his men by helping man the Napoleons which he turned on the attackers. After several unsuccessful forays against Pelham's murderous point-blank fire, the decimated Federals broke off the fight and withdrew.

While the Horse Artillery beat off this attack on the vital supply wagons, General Hill's "Light Division" absorbed terrific punishment from wave after wave of enemy troops that General Pope had ordered to crush General Jackson's left wing and then roll up the rest of his two-mile line. "Powell" Hill's tough veterans met each assault with a shower of lead followed by bayonet charges which cleared the front. Before long, 4,000 enemy dead and wounded lay heaped in front of the railroad embankment.

But General Hill, raging up and down his lines in a red battle-shirt, was not content to hold the enemy at bay. He now decided to take the offensive and deliver a bold counterattack. He sent a courier to Major Pelham requesting him to bring forward the Horse Artillery to support the attack. Pelham immediately advanced his guns to a ridge overlooking the enemy artillery at Groveton.

For two hours Pelham's guns blazed away at General Pope's

massed batteries which returned a withering fire on Pelham's front and flank. However, Pelham continued to hold his own against this superior firepower until the ammunition for five of his six guns was exhausted. Turning to Jim Breathed, he said: "Take these five guns out of range to the rear." And to Sergeant Hoxton he gave the order: "Gallop to General Hill and ask him to send me reinforcements."

Then for twenty minutes Pelham sighted and directed the fire of his remaining gun which spiritedly answered the deafening enemy barrage. By then the ammunition was down to the last two rounds, and Sergeant Hoxton returned to report that he had been unable to find General Hill. Disappointed, Pelham shouted: "We'll have to retire, men. Limber up!"

Nightfall found the lines about where they had been at daybreak. General Jackson had repulsed six separate attacks, giving Generals Lee and Longstreet time to march from Thoroughfare Gap and take position on the right.

Unaware that the Army of Northern Virginia had been reunited under General Lee, General Pope boastfully wired Washington: "Today we drove them from the field." And while his exhausted bluecoats spread out around a galaxy of campfires, the Federal commander issued orders for "the vigorous pursuit of the enemies" whom he said must be destroyed.

By contrast, the Confederate lines were dark and quiet to deceive General Pope into believing that only a picket line remained. In this calm atmosphere General Lee held a council of war in his tent. On pushing aside the tent flaps at General Lee's headquarters, General Stuart was greeted by Generals Lee, Longstreet and Jackson who were seated on camp-stools. Turning to "Stonewall," "Jeb" remarked: "I hear that you had a rough tussle with General Pope to-day."

"That's correct," General Jackson replied quietly, "but with the help of Almighty God we repulsed them. And if you have no objection, General, I'd like to borrow Major Pelham and the Horse Artillery again to-morrow."

"Certainly," Stuart answered generously, "just so long as you don't keep him permanently."

Not realizing that "Jeb" was jesting, "Stonewall" responded seriously: "Of course you may have him back after the battle. But if you have another Pelham, please give him to me."

At this point General Lee broke in to outline his plans for the morrow.

"Gentlemen," he began with a faint smile, "I have released some prisoners who are well supplied with planted information that our army is retreating. This should bestir General Pope to push his army in this direction tomorrow. He will be surprised to encounter our entire army in position to meet him. I trust you will give him a warm reception."

"My ammunition is low," mused General Jackson, "but the men have been gathering rocks to hurl, and we can always give them the bayonet."

"Old Pete" Longstreet, the heavy-set Dutchman, scratched his bushy brown beard and added with a grin, "General Jackson, if they press you too hard just send word to me and my troops will run to your assistance."

"Yes," chimed in General Stuart, "and don't forget that the cavalry stands ready to guard the flanks and harass any enemy attacks."

Rising from his stool, General Lee rose to his full height and brought the council of war to a close by stating: "Gentlemen, we have frustrated the enemy's attempt to annihilate General Jackson. General Pope, believing that General Jackson is still isolated and fleeing, probably will advance and attack again tomorrow. If he does, I plan to counterattack with all of our available forces—infantry, artillery, and cavalry. Let us make our preparations accordingly."

After this conference "Stonewall" rode along his lines where battle-hardened veterans lay sleeping without blankets and with empty cartridge cases for pillows. Slightly behind the front line he came upon Pelham who was busily engaged in replenishing the ammunition for his battery. Drawing rein, "Stonewall" watched approvingly as Pelham assisted his men load the shells into the caissons.

When Pelham was finished, General Jackson said, "Major, you are to serve with me again tomorrow. You will hold the Horse Artillery in readiness to go to the relief of any point that is threatened. Our ammunition is low so reserve your supply for emergency use only."

"Yes, General," replied Pelham saluting. Then as "Stonewall" disappeared in the shadows, Pelham stretched out on the dewy ground and immediately dropped off to sleep.

Saturday, August 30th, dawned bright. Pelham rose early and inspected his battery before gulping down his ration of bacon and hard crackers. Then he and Jim Breathed mounted their horses and galloped to the front. Peering over the parapet they saw bayonets glistening in the distant woodland and heard the creak of enemy guns as they rumbled into position opposite the Confederate left.

Eager to get a closer view of the enemy's movements, Pelham pulled out his field-glasses and watched the bluecoats march and countermarch. Handing the glasses to Breathed, he commented: "Have a look, Jim. It appears to me that General Pope is massing his troops to spearhead another attack against General Jackson's line."

"I think you're right," Jim agreed, "and I only wish we could stall them by throwing a few shells in their midst."

"It's a big temptation," Pelham admitted, "but General Jackson has ordered me to save our ammunition for close range work where each shell will find its mark."

During the morning and early afternoon General Jackson's long gray line lay concealed behind the railroad embankment awaiting the enemy thunderbolt. Finally, about three o'clock General Pope thrust forward a swarm of skirmishers followed by three interminable lines of infantry in close ranks. Close on the heels of the infantry lumbered the Union batteries.

Twenty-thousand smartly-clad bluecoats swept across the waving meadows as though on parade. On approaching the railroad embankment Pope's skirmishers were surprised to encounter a heavy picket line which fell back slowly to allow "Stonewall's" concealed guns to take careful aim on the front regiments.

Suddenly, Confederate buglers pierced the air all along the line with notes calling the infantry to arms. General Jackson's forty guns and Pelham's mobile artillery immediately opened on the advancing troops at close range. The Yankees, startled to find a strong Confederate force still on the field, halted and then fell back to re-form their broken ranks.

As they did so Pelham turned his devastating fire of twelve shells per minute on a thicket behind which enemy reinforcements were gathering. In the face of this rapid, concentrated firepower, General Pope's brave men resumed their offensive against General Jackson's line. This time a mounted Federal officer waving his saber led the determined assault which carried the enemy flags to within ten paces of the Confederate front line. Thrilled at the spectacle of such courage, Pelham yelled at his comrades: "Don't shoot him! Capture him!" But at that instant the gallant Federal officer reeled from his horse with a bullet through his head.

General Jackson's men stubbornly contested the enemy's attacks with a storm of shell and shrapnel. When their ammunition ran out, the graycoats hurled stones and grappled with the oncomers in hand-to-hand combat. Pelham continued to tear holes in the supporting lines with each puff of gunsmoke, but he was powerless to break up the fierce front-line struggle for fear of hitting his comrades.

After two hours of fierce in-fighting, General Pope ordered a "do-or-die" assault against the Confederate left. When the full fury of this drive struck Jackson's front, "Stonewall" dispatched a courier to General Longstreet requesting him to rush a division to bolster the hard-pressed defenders. The messenger found "Old Pete" calmly watching the course of the battle from a hill at the intersection of his line with "Stonewall's."

"Old Pete" had noticed that as the enemy lines advanced against General Jackson they exposed their left flank to fire from the Confederate right. Realizing that his artillery could relieve the pressure on Jackson faster than a division could, he turned to an aide and instructed him to order Colonel Stephen D. Lee's batteries forward. Within a few minutes whistling shells from Colonel Lee's eighteen guns were mowing down the bluecoats with scythe-like efficiency.

When enemy survivors in General Pope's second and third lines fled under this barrage, the front line Yankees turned to follow their comrades only to expose their backs to the raking fire of Pelham's guns.

"Fire fast and low," Pelham yelled, his face aglow with excitement now that the enemy attack was broken. Ten minutes after Colonel Lee's artillery had gone into action nary a bluecoat remained on General Jackson's front.

Then, in unison, General Lee's 50,000 graycoats raised the piercing Rebel Yell and dashed after the remnants of General Pope's army. Along a four-mile front the frenzied gray lines swept forward, their bayonets glittering in the sunlight and red banners billowing in the breeze. Pelham, of course, joined in the irresistible counterattack. With his guns he darted from sector to sector spraying canister on the retreating enemy troops,

then changing to grape to break up islands of organized resistance around a cannon or two.

Darkness finally ended the pursuit which had forced General
Pope's army back to the heights bordering Bull Run. The Federal commander who had boasted of seeing the "backs of the
enemy," now had his own front broken and his shattered rear
within a day's march of Washington. His unsuccessful campaign against General Lee had cost him over 14,000 casualties,
30 cannon, and 20,000 small arms.

Although General Pope's army was defeated it was not destroyed. Hence, although it rained heavily the day after the
Battle of Second Manassas, General Lee sent his reliable Jack-
son-Stuart-Pelham combination sweeping around the Federal
army to intercept its retreat to the defenses of Washington.

Along the muddy trails victorious gray columns plodded in
search of the enemy who only three months ago had been
knocking at the gates of Richmond. By nightfall the weary
pursuers reached the village of Pleasant Valley where General
Jackson halted for the night. Some of Pelham's cannoneers
grumbled because the commissary wagons had been delayed
and would not be up in time to issue supper rations.

"Come with me, boys," Pelham said cheerily, "and we'll see
if the neighboring farmers have some spare grub for us."

As Pelham suspected, the friendly Virginians were overjoyed
at the opportunity to take the famished, mud-spattered lads
into their homes and feed them the best meal their own meager
cupboards could provide. During supper the boys described
the battle in which they had just whipped "Pope's Yankee
army."

Jean, the Creole gunner, started to tell his hosts in broken
English about the deeds of his hero, Major Pelham, whereupon
John blushed a bright crimson and smilingly cut short this
kind of talk by saying: "Now, Jean, you know that all I do is

give orders—you brave fellows do all of the hard fighting."

After supper the party moved to the living-room where the soldiers enjoyed a song-fest around the blazing fireplace. As they sang loudly if not harmoniously, Pelham's thoughts turned homeward to Alabama. If only they could overtake and destroy General Pope's army before it reached Washington this terrible conflict would end and everyone could return home to enjoy his family and resume a useful life.

At daybreak on an overcast September 1, Pelham led the advance down the Little River Turnpike toward Washington. Beside him rode General Stuart and behind them rumbled a fat, pear-shaped Blakely gun hitched to a caisson. Late in the afternoon as the head of the column approached a hamlet known as Chantilly, Pelham called General Stuart's attention to the smoking ruins of what had been a stately colonial mansion.

Angered by this sight, "Jeb" snorted: "Major, it certainly looks as though the enemy has razed this building on his retreat."

"Yes," Pelham mused, "but it's odd that in their haste to get to Washington the Yanks should take time out to burn homes unless there was a good reason."

"True," "Jeb" agreed, "but what possible reason could there be for this burning?"

"It's only a guess," Pelham answered, "but if the enemy set up an ambush ahead, he would want to have this mansion levelled so that his artillery could have a clear sweep of the approaches."

"You may be right," Stuart said excitedly, drawing rein and holding up his hand for the column to halt. Turning to Pelham, he said, "Bring your Blakely to the side of the hill on your left and open fire on the woods to the right of the turnpike. If there's an ambush we'll flush the bluecoats out."

Under General Stuart's admiring eyes, Pelham swiftly un-limbered the Blakely and opened fire. Sure enough, the first shot brought out a swarm of enemy sharpshooters who started firing on the gunners.

"You've flushed the Yankees out," Stuart cried jubilantly.

"Yes," Pelham shouted back, "but we don't have any canister to shoot their infantry at close range."

"Fire a few rounds and then rejoin the main column," Stuart replied.

By the time Pelham had executed this order, the enemy had brought up two divisions to contest the Confederate advance. Just as the opposing forces clashed, a drenching rainstorm ac-companied by thunderclaps and streaks of lightning broke in full fury. During the ensuing struggle one Confederate offi-cer asked General Jackson's permission to withdraw his men from the firing line, "because my ammunition is wet." Irritated at this flimsy excuse to avoid a fight, "Stonewall" replied stern-ly, "The enemy's ammunition is just as wet—stay where you are!"

For over an hour the two lines wavered back and forth— one side gaining an advantage only to be pushed back by the other. Pelham maintained a steady deadly fire throughout the battle which ended suddenly when the Federals withdrew fol-lowing the deaths of two brave divisional commanders, Gen-erals Kearney and Stevens. Able and colorful Phil Kearny was shot as he rode into General Jackson's line thinking it was his own.

The next day Stuart and Pelham skirmished with the retreat-ing bluecoats as far as Fairfax Court House. Here General Stuart lost his temper when he saw the trail of smoking barns and homes destroyed by the enemy for no legitimate reason.

"Bring up your guns," he told Pelham, "and pepper those arsonists."

Pelham's parting shots were still ringing in General Pope's ears when he reached Washington, where he was relieved of his command and succeeded by General George "Little Mac" McClellan—General Lee's former antagonist.

Stirring them up

Battle of Antietam

CHAPTER VI

"Artillery Hell"

WHILE General McClellan rallied and reorganized General Pope's shattered divisions which hovered in the fortifications around Washington, General Lee made plans for an immediate Northern invasion. As Washington was too strongly fortified for a direct assault, General Lee decided to march up the Potomac River, cross it, and head northward through Maryland. This maneuver would draw "Little Mac" and his army after the Army of Northern Virginia and away from Virginia soil which lay barren after a year of occupation and fighting.

Three days after the engagement at Chantilly, General Stuart headed the advance toward the Potomac. At his side rode Major Pelham, followed by three batteries of the Horse Artillery which "Jeb" proudly wrote his wife, "has won imperishable laurels."

Behind the cavalry marched 53,000 ragged soldiers, many of whom were barefoot and clad in captured enemy clothes. Even the supply wagons bore the insignia, U.S.A. But what the lean Confederates lacked in clothing and food, they more than made up for in spirit. They had absolute confidence that commanders such as Lee, Jackson, Longstreet, Stuart and Pelham would lead them to ultimate victory.

By nightfall the Horse Artillery reached Goose Creek near Leesburg. Other units also arrived and soon the entire countryside was illuminated by campfires around which the soldiers sang, cheered, and shouted "huzzah." John Pelham took time from his duties to write his parents:

"We whipped General Pope last week at Manassas. Now General Lee is leading us into Northern territory. Tomorrow we'll cross the Potomac and enter Maryland, where they tell us a lot of men are anxious to join our cause. I understand that General Jackson wants to invade Pennsylvania in order to strike the coal mines and railroads so as to cripple the enemy's industry and transportation. If all goes well I hope that the war will be over soon and then we can all be together again—at least that is my prayer."

Late the next day Pelham limbered up his guns and hauled them to White's Ford on the broad Potomac which General Jackson's troops were then fording. Seeing that it would be several hours before the Horse Artillery could follow this procession, Pelham ordered his men to unhitch the teams and let them graze while the crews rested on the bank. Pelham joined Breathed on a knoll to view the spectacle in the river. As "Stonewall's" veterans reached the water they rolled up their frayed trouser legs and plunged into the cold Potomac which at this point was about two-and-one-half feet deep. Late in the afternoon the setting sun cast its fiery rays on the shiny muskets and tattered battle flags held high above the sparkling surface of the river.

Suddenly an officer on a cream-colored mare splashed into the river and rode beside the troops to midstream. Here he drew rein and doffed his familiar kepi hat to his devoted troops who shouted the Rebel Yell and cheered "Hurrah for General Stonewall Jackson." A regimental band on the far shore caught the spirit of the occasion and struck up the lilting song, "Maryland, My Maryland."

About midnight Pelham got his guns into line for the crossing. "Keep the muzzles pointed up so as to keep water out of the barrels," he cautioned. When he caught sight of gunners sitting on the caissons, he shouted: "No one is to ride across on the caissons as the added weight will make it easier to get stuck."

The men obeyed and walked behind the guns and caissons, putting their shoulders to the carriage wheels when the horses stalled in deep water. On reaching the Maryland shore Pelham led his men to a grove where they bivouacked. Next morning the Horse Artillery joined the cavalry and headed toward Frederick.

Along the way groups of farmers and their families gathered beside the road to gape at the passing army which had become so famous. Although children waved, their elders displayed neither enthusiasm nor hostility to the troops in faded gray uniforms. Noticing the neutral attitude of the citizens, Pelham rode close to General Stuart and commented: "These people look disappointed and surprised to see that we look like a mob of tramps instead of resembling the neatly-uniformed bluecoats we whip every time in battle."

"Yes," "Jeb" laughed, "our hungry, ragged appearance may scare their young men from joining up with us. They probably wonder how on earth an army like ours can possibly win victories."

Nevertheless, the farmers generously allowed the famished graycoats to help themselves to their corn which was ripening in the fields. And for the next two weeks the invading Army of

Northern Virginia lived mainly on green corn with an occasional helping of potatoes and fruit.

Just before reaching Poolesville, the head of the cavalry column bumped into a small force of enemy troopers. "Jeb" instantly charged, whereupon thirty stunned bluecoats threw down their arms and surrendered while their comrades fled.

Impressed by this display of dash, a number of young men in Poolesville saddled their horses and volunteered their services to General Stuart. Two of the village shopkeepers offered to join up if they could sell out their stock. On hearing this, "Jeb's" veterans jammed their stores to buy up all of the food, clothing and novelties of their new Confederates. During this "closing out" sale, Pelham called Jim Breathed's attention to Heros von Borcke elbowing his huge bulk through the crowded general merchandise store to purchase "zom uf yoor best seegars" which he lit and smoked as he fumbled in his wallet for a Confederate bill.

"Heros smokes enough cigars to keep the army warm in winter," jested Breathed.

"And did you ever see a cigar look as tiny as it does when he puffs on one?" added Pelham.

While the infantry encamped around Frederick—where General Lee issued a proclamation inviting the people of Maryland to join the Confederacy—Stuart and Pelham established headquarters at Urbana, a small town seven miles southeast of Frederick. "Jeb" immediately posted his three cavalry brigades along a north-south line to screen the army from any sally General McClellan might make from the national capital only forty miles to the east.

With their troops carefully posted, "Jeb's" staff officers eagerly accepted the hospitality of Mr. Cockey, a local sympathizer, who invited them to make their headquarters in his spacious shady yard. Here they slept with boots on and horses saddled for instant action. But when "Little Mac" showed no disposition to attack, Stuart's gay swains occupied their spare time making friends with their host and his lovely daughters, Martha and Virginia.

General Stuart and Major von Borcke particularly enjoyed the company of Ann Cockey, charming young cousin of Martha and Virginia. Ann was a New Yorker who happened to be visiting her Maryland relatives at the time of General Lee's invasion, and she decided to stay on to enjoy the excitement. Although she was a Northerner, Ann favored the Confederate cause. Consequently, "Jeb" teased her about "deserting" the Yankees to become the "New York Rebel." Heros, with his romantic inclinations, flirted shamelessly with Ann—tenderly patting her silken blonde hair with his enormous leathery paws.

Pelham and Breathed double-dated with Martha and Virginia. Each evening after supper they would stroll through the apple orchards discussing everything from the future course of the war to life in Alabama. Pelham was completely at ease with pretty, dark-haired Virginia who proved to be an attentive listener and stimulating conversationalist.

"War is such a horrible thing," she said one evening as they were speculating about the coming campaign. "Don't you ever get scared in the heat of a battle, John?"

"Sure, we all get butterflies here," he answered frankly pointing to his stomach, "but we forget our fears in doing our duties once the battle begins. As the saying goes, I don't believe the bullet has been made that has my name on it. God has seen fit to protect me so far and that's all I can ask for."

One day after making his round of inspection with the staff, General Stuart exclaimed, "Boys, how about varying the routine by holding a ball tomorrow night in the deserted academy buildings on the edge of Urbana? I'll arrange for music and the rest of you help Heros decorate the hall."

Without dismounting, the mammoth Prussian rode into town accompanied by Pelham, Breathed and several others on "Jeb's" staff. On entering the musty red-brick building that had recently been used as a school for girls, Heros sniffed the stale air and snorted, "Vee moost air thees out if vee vant it to be roomantic-like vor zee ladees at der dance."

While his companions hastened to pry open the cobwebbed windows, von Borcke scratched his head for ideas as to how he could decorate the drab interior. Suddenly his stern mouth turned into a grin, and he beckoned his assistants to join him. "Vot do you vellows theenk aboot decorating der hall mit our bright regimental vlags?" he asked.

"Just the thing," Pelham agreed, "they'll cover up the bare walls and provide a dash of color at the same time."

When the decoration committee left the academy, a throng of townspeople pressed around von Borcke, cheering him and tossing bouquets before him. Pelham, curious as to why the citizens were showering such attentions on von Borcke, asked one of the bystanders what all the fuss was about, and was told, "Why we're honoring General "Stonewall" Jackson, of course." Pelham chuckled at the thought that the villagers apparently thought the famous General must have a build to match his reputation. All the while Heros graciously accepted their favors, and later turned over the flowers to his committee to be used in decorating the ballroom.

Heros von Borcke's decoration committee spent all of the following day sweeping out the hall, dusting the chairs and woodwork, and draping Confederate flags and regimental banners around the walls and bandstand. Lighting arrangements, which the romantic officers kept to a minimum, consisted of two brass candelabra posted behind the band to illuminate the sheet music. Pelham added a festive note by hanging colored lanterns over the entrance doors.

Much to the officers' delight a romantic full moon peeked over the horizon after dark. Pelham and Breathed carefully donned their full-dress uniforms and called at Colonel Cockey's home for Virginia and Martha whom they escorted to the hall. Shortly after their arrival, Heros von Borcke in all his be-medalled splendor entered with the "New York Rebel" on his arm.

As a precaution in case of attack the officers came fully armed, and aides picketed their horses in the schoolyard. Inside the academy the young cavaliers stacked their sabers against the walls so that they could dance freely without their scabbards banging each other.

When the dashing officers in gray and their radiant partners in hoop-skirted crinoline gowns had all arrived, "Jeb" mounted the bandstand and announced that he would lead the Grand March while the Eighteenth Mississippi band played "Dixie." With that, the gay affair got underway, and for several hours the cares of war were forgotten as couples skipped to the Virginia Reel, polkaed, and waltzed rhythmically to such sentimental strains as "Somebody's Darling," "Lorena," and "The Girl I Left Behind Me."

While dancing the latter number, Virginia coyly asked, with a twinkle in her appealing brown eyes, "John, how many girls did you leave back home in Alabama?"

John blushed at this blunt question, but answered truthfully, "Ginny, the only girls I left behind in good old Alabamy are my dear mother and sister Betty."

John was about to tell his tall beautiful companion what he thought of Maryland girls when the dreamy music was interrupted by the distant bark of a cannon followed by the rattle of musketry. At this instant an excited courier dashed into the hall and loudly informed General Stuart that enemy troops were attacking the outposts manned by the First North Carolina.

"Jeb" instantly reassured the young ladies that there was no cause for alarm, but that the officers would have to leave for a short time to teach a lesson to some impertinent Yankees who apparently thought they could shoot their way into the dance. As "Jeb" spoke the musicians exchanged their instruments for muskets and Pelham hastily bowed to Virginia, promising that he would return just as soon as the pesky Yankees were silenced.

Outside the building General Stuart and his officers jumped on their horses and rode pell-mell to the sound of firing. A few miles east of Urbana they found the North Carolina picket line holding its own against the heavy fire of General McClellan's advance units. "Jeb" ordered Pelham to disperse the bluecoats with a few rounds of canister while the small squad of cavalrymen raised the Rebel Yell and shouted orders to imaginary troops so as to mislead the enemy into believing that a large Confederate force was at hand. The ruse worked, and within a few minutes nary a shot was heard from "Little Mac's" retreating soldiers.

After this brief affair, the officers returned to the academy where they resumed their dancing—giving wide berth to von Borcke who swung his partners around like rag dolls. Dancing continued until dawn when wounded arrived on stretchers, whereupon the young ladies acted as nurses in caring for the moaning, bleeding boys. Seeing his "New York Rebel" tenderly comforting a suffering foot-soldier, von Borcke exclaimed: "I don't theenk I mind getting vounded meinself eef I could get ein sveet nurse like dot."

Two days after this memorable evening, General Lee ordered his army to head westward toward Hagerstown, the city which he planned to use as a base of operations for the invasion of Pennsylvania. Before departing, Pelham, Breathed, and von Borcke reluctantly bade farewell to the Cockey sisters and

the "New York Rebel" who had made their stay at Urbana
so pleasant.

On the march General Stuart's cavalry brought up the rear,
forming a screen between General Lee's infantry and General
McClellan's army which moved into Frederick after the Confederates left. When the last of General Lee's supply wagons
had rumbled through Turner's Gap at South Mountain, twelve
miles west of Frederick, General Stuart posted cavalry to guard
the pass. As an added precaution he dispatched Major Pelham together with a battery of the Horse Artillery and a cavalry detachment under Colonel Tom Rosser (Pelham's close
friend and classmate at West Point) to Fox's Gap a mile to the
south. Confederate possession of Fox's Gap was necessary to
prevent the force at Turner's Gap from being outflanked. In
addition, this position commanded a sweep of the approaches
over which the enemy would soon come.

And come the bluecoats did. Cautious "Little Mac," who
normally advanced at a snail's pace, suddenly pursued the invaders after one of his soldiers found a copy of General Lee's
Special Orders 191 wrapped around three cigars lying on the
ground in Frederick. These orders gave the exact locations and
intentions of General Lee's scattered troops. Of greatest importance was the vital information that General Jackson was on
his way with half of the Army of Northern Virginia to capture a strong Federal garrison at Harper's Ferry. General
McClellan realized that if he moved fast he might do what
General Pope had failed to do—destroy General Lee's divided
army one-half at a time.

During the night of September 13 a civilian on horseback
dashed up to General Stuart's outposts at Turner's Gap. When
challenged by one of the guards, he replied that he was a friend
from Frederick with important information for the cavalry
chief. Allowed to pass, he blurted out the story to "Jeb" that

"Little Mac" had obtained a copy of General Lee's orders and was rushing westward toward South Mountain to overtake the Army of Northern Virginia.

General Stuart forwarded this intelligence to General Lee who halted "Old Pete" Longstreet's column at Hagerstown and countermarched it to "Jeb" Stuart's assistance. However, by the following morning General Stuart's cavalry, the Horse Artillery, and 3,000 men of General D. H. Hill's division were all that stood in the way of General McClellan's vast army of 90,000 bluecoats who were preparing to batter their way through the passes of South Mountain and cut off General Longstreet's divisions from those with "Stonewall" Jackson.

At Fox's Gap Pelham stationed his guns in the edge of woods which overlooked the slopes up which the enemy was massing for a charge. Nearby, Tom Rosser had dismounted his cavalry and posted them behind a stone wall. General Samuel Garland of Hill's division also arrived with five North Carolina regiments and a battery of artillery. These troops fanned out on either side of the Old Sharpsburg Road which ran through the gap.

While awaiting the expected attack, Pelham instructed his gunners to fire low as the enemy would be coming uphill and it was easy to fire over their heads. Then catching sight of the double lines of bluecoats stretched out in a solid column to the distant horizon, he stood in his stirrups and addressed his gunners:

"Men of the Horse Artillery, the safety of General Lee's wagon trains and the security of the whole army depend on our holding off the enemy until help can arrive. We must hold on at any cost. Now, to battery!"

At 9 A.M. waves of bluecoats swarmed upon the defending graycoats from all sides. Outnumbered three-to-one, the gallant North Carolina regiments fought stubbornly, supported by Pelham's Napoleon guns which alternately turned their fire on the enemy's infantry and heavy guns. Suddenly, a Yankee sharpshooter felled General Garland with a well-aimed bullet. But his leaderless men fought on gamely until their ammunition was exhausted before they surrendered.

Sensing disaster, Pelham conferred with Tom Rosser about the situation. "Tom," he said, "if your men can make a strong demonstration on the front as though you are about to charge, my boys will blast a hole through the enemy on our rear and we'll all dash to another position up the hill a short distance."

Rosser was game and quickly succeeded in bluffing the enemy into believing his men were about to attack with newly arrived reinforcements. When the bluecoats fell back to receive Rosser's charge, Pelham's guns opened a gap in the rear through which the Horse Artillery and Rosser's troopers poured. Taking position further up the hill, Pelham's battery sprayed their would-be captors with such a storm of shot and canister that the Federal commander thought heavy reinforcements had arrived, and he called off the attack for the remainder of the morning.

All afternoon Pelham played his guns on the persistent enemy infantry who repeatedly tried to gain control of the pass. Finally at dusk, the tall Texans of General Hood's division arrived and help beat off the last enemy thrust of the day.

All along the front the thin gray line had held at the fearful cost of 1,800 brave men who lay dead and wounded on the slopes of South Mountain. General Stuart had feared that Pelham might have been among those killed or captured with General Garland's men. He was naturally overjoyed, therefore, to find his missing protégé alive and unhurt after this bitter struggle. Grasping Pelham's hand tightly, "Jeb" greeted Pelham warmly: "Major, I'm delighted to see you. I heard a report this afternoon that you had been cut off and surrounded."

"We were," Pelham grinned, "but Colonel Rosser and the Horse Artillery somehow managed to cut their way out and keep fighting."

That night General Lee abandoned his plan for invading Pennsylvania and decided instead to reunite his divided army at the nearby town of Sharpsburg where he would take on this aggressive, rejuvenated army of General McClellan. On the march Pelham's battery served as the rearguard which kept enemy patrols at bay with canister barrages.

When Pelham reached Sharpsburg with the Horse Artillery, General Longstreet was disposing his troops along the high ground overlooking the rolling cornfields and orchards between the winding Potomac and Antietam Creek. Pelham stationed his guns on a hill north of the town opposite masses of blue-coated infantrymen who were moving into position behind the drowsy Antietam.

"They must have at least twice as many troops in line as we do," Jim Breathed observed grimly.

"If they attack soon we'll be in a tight spot," Pelham admitted, "but General Stuart informs me that General Jackson has captured over eleven thousand Yankees at Harper's Ferry. He is now hurrying to rejoin us and should arrive shortly."

About noon General Jackson's "foot cavalry" strode into view and took position on General Longstreet's left. Late in the afternoon large bodies of enemy troops and guns appeared to be massing for an advance against the left of General Lee's line. Pelham discouraged their aggressiveness with a fusillade of grape and canister until General Lee rode up and told Pelham to hold his fire as the army's supply of ammunition was low.

Realizing that "Little Mac" was simply probing the strength of the Confederate lines, General Lee cautioned Pelham: "Save your fire, Major, for the critical full-scale battle we'll probably

fight tomorrow. Then we'll need all of our ammunition for close range work where every shell will have to count."

After dark General Stuart directed Pelham to pull his four serviceable guns out of line and move them to a knobby ridge on the extreme left beyond General Jackson's flank. The cavalry chief selected this position which bordered the Potomac, because it formed a natural anchor for the Confederate left from which troopers and artillery could either resist an enemy flank attack or mount a counter-offensive should the opportunity arise.

While Pelham was cooking his half ration of beef, von Borcke rode up and shared his knapsack which was overflowing with home-cooked food that some of the local women insisted he take. The two officers had just finished this delicious meal when a drizzling rain began to fall. Pelham invited Heros to share his "shelter" consisting of a nearby haystack that provided the most comfortable bed they had enjoyed in many a moon. And despite a brisk exchange of fire on the picket lines, the weary comrades were soon fast asleep.

At 3 A.M. the roll of drums awakened Pelham who in turn roused his gunners and ordered them to ready their guns for instant action. It was still dark when the rattle of musketry was heard from across the Hagerstown Turnpike opposite General Jackson's troops in the cornfield. Remembering General Lee's advice, Pelham cautioned his men, "Hold your fire until the enemy comes into full view!"

Shortly after 5 o'clock the darkness lifted and revealed a solid mass of bluecoats advancing against General Jackson's front. Scouts quickly identified them as belonging to General Hooker's First Corps, 12,500 strong. Any concern Pelham may have felt about the unequal odds was overshadowed by his realization that the enemy was unaware that the Horse Artillery stood poised to enfilade his ranks from the side as the bluecoats moved against the Confederates now nervously fingering their muskets amidst the cornstalks.

The moment the Federal 20-pounder Parrott guns opened fire on General Jackson's men, Pelham in his ringing voice gave the order for which his artillerists had been impatiently awaiting. "Fire!" he shouted, whereupon the battery blazed in unison. The first salvo felled sixteen front-line bluecoats, but the surprised enemy troops bravely closed ranks and pushed ahead through the morning mist.

With the battle joined, the air was soon full of whistling lead and artillery thunderclaps. Pelham's fire tore such gaps in the enemy's lines that Colonel Hunt, the able Federal artillerist who had taught Pelham gunnery at West Point, turned his heavy fire on the Horse Artillery with destructive accuracy. Most of the draft horses used to draw Pelham's guns and caissons were hit and had to be shot in the head to end their misery.

To avoid further losses Pelham ordered his men to change their range to 800 yards and aim for Colonel Hunt's batteries. A lively exchange ensued during which the opposing guns arched their shells over a large farmhouse between the lines. As the fusillade raged back and forth Pelham was alarmed to see women and children stream out of the house which sheltered them from the fire and race frantically toward the battle lines. Pelham and his men shouted and waved at them to go back to the house as the gunners were firing over it and would not harm them. But the frightened women insisted on leaving the house. Fearful lest they be struck by stray bullets, Pelham ordered his battery to cease firing, whereupon Colonel Hunt followed suit. Pelham then mounted his horse, and, accompanied by his staff and some of General Stuart's officers, rode out to escort the crying children and their panic-stricken mothers to safety.

On returning to his battery after completing this errand of

mercy, Pelham discovered that General Jackson was so impressed with the effective manner in which Pelham was engaging the enemy, that "Stonewall" had sent him fifteen guns from other units to form an artillery battalion. At this juncture General Jackson certainly needed all the firepower that could be mustered. General Hooker's First Corps was now driving ahead furiously without counting the cost. After two hours of fierce see-saw fighting the bluecoats had forced the defenders back half a mile, killed many Confederate officers, and thinned the gray ranks to a token force. The musketry exchange crackled so furiously that every cornstalk in the thirty-acre cornfield was cut down—and on this "carpet" 1,700 gallant defenders had fallen in straight rows as though mowed down by a scythe.

To relieve this relentless pressure on General Jackson's line, Pelham ordered the nineteen guns now under his command to lay down a barrage of double canister. This spread such destruction among General Hooker's troops and six batteries that the Federal commander dispatched troops under General Abner Doubleday (who twenty years before the war invented the national game of baseball) to quiet "those infernal cannon." Pelham managed to pepper and disperse this force with canister in a free-for-all in which Jean, the begrimed Creole sponger, deftly toppled a Federal officer on horseback who charged into the Napoleon Detachment.

By now it was 7:30 in the morning, and General Hooker's offensive had stalled. While the enemy caught his breath and brought up General Mansfield's 10,000 fresh troops of the Twelfth Corps, "Stonewall" calmly ordered up General Hood's Texas division, 2,000 strong, and General "Old Jube" Early's brigade of 1,000 Virginians to reinforce his perilously thin front.

While these sweating troops in faded gray uniforms quick-stepped to fill the ranks of their fallen comrades, Pelham took the opportunity to change position. He saw that since the Confederate left had fallen back his batteries could concentrate their fire more effectively on the advancing enemy if they were moved down closer to "Stonewall's" flank. After securing General Stuart's approval, Pelham shouted the order in a voice now hoarse: "Limber! To the right, gallop!" Within a few minutes all nineteen guns were in position on a plateau from which their fire could sweep the enemy if he dared advance further.

And dare advance he did. But as the Yankees pushed ahead over the dead and wounded in the cornfield, Pelham's five batteries showered them with a murderous fire of grape and canister that surprised them as they had not seen Pelham change position. One bluecoat who saw 4,000 of his comrades slaughtered during these assaults, described Pelham's devastating fire as "artillery hell."

Shortly after this second attack was launched, "Fightin' Joe" Hooker was wounded and bewhiskered General "Daddy" Mansfield was killed. Nevertheless, the indomitable bluecoats kept coming on against the force General Jackson had assembled to stem the tide.

Assailed by infantry fire in front and Pelham's guns on their flank, the advancing Federals gradually ground to a halt and then withdrew. Pelham, grateful for the cease-fire and beamingly proud of his men, ordered the exhausted gun-crews to stretch out on the ground and rest while he kept an eye on the enemy's activities. Before long he blinked his eyes at an alarming spectacle. Marching up the slopes from Antietam Creek in three long lines flanked by heavy artillery, was General "Old Bull" Sumner's Second Corps, 18,000 strong.

In a roaring voice that carried the length of his lines, "Old Bull" ordered the troops to attack General Jackson. With banners flying in the breeze the bluecoats swept forward against "Stonewall's" invincible veterans awaiting the attack in front of a quaint small white building known as the Dunkard Church. Snapping out of his trance, Pelham shouted: "On your feet men, and to your posts!"

Just before General Sumner's divisions collided with "Stonewall's" line, Pelham's guns blasted their flanks with a merciless fire. Again and again the cannoneers loaded, rammed, fired and sponged the Blakelys and Napoleons which spread havoc among the bluecoats. And again Colonel Hunt directed a blistering fire from his hundred rifled guns on the other side of the Antietam. Pelham immediately moved his guns from hill to hill to keep losses to a minimum.

As the Federals crossed the Hagerstown road and proceeded through a wooded area, strong Confederate reinforcements arrived from the right of General Lee's line and ambushed the unwary Yankees who lost over 2,200 within a few minutes.

All along General Jackson's front the bloodied defenders raised the Rebel Yell and fell upon "Old Bull's" Twelfth Corps which had been frustrated in its headlong attack. "Stonewall's" fierce counterattack supported by Pelham's smoking guns quickly drove the bluecoats back to their starting line.

It was now almost noon. Since daybreak the vastly outnumbered graycoats had repulsed wave after wave of bluecoats in a struggle which left the front covered with dead and horribly mangled wounded who cried pitifully, "Water, for God's sake, water."

Would the relentless Federals again attack the Confederate left? "Stonewall" Jackson thought not. Sitting thoughtfully on his horse, one leg thrown casually over the pommel, he sucked a lemon as was his habit when planning the next move. Almost to himself he said, "They have done their worst." Then turning to "Jeb" Stuart, he said, "General, I want you and

Major Pelham to reconnoiter the enemy's right. If you find the situation favorable, I want to organize a force of 5,000 to overwhelm this wing and drive General McClellan into the Potomac."

General Stuart hastily gathered up a few riders while Pelham selected three of his own guns together with Captain Bill Poague's Rockbridge Battery which consisted of four smoothbore 6-pounder guns named Matthew, Mark, Luke and John, because—so said their crew—"they spoke a powerful language." Taking a roundabout path to avoid detection, Pelham led his seven guns to a patch of trees less than 500 yards from thirty formidable cannon which guarded the right flank of "Little Mac's" army near the Potomac.

To his men's amazement, Pelham ordered them to open fire on this massed battery. But when the captain of the Rockbridge Battery protested against attacking such an overwhelming force at close range with only seven guns, Pelham laughingly replied, "Oh, we'll only stir them up to see if they're in condition to fight—then we'll slip away."

And stir them up he did. The first salvo brought an answer from all thirty guns which fired toward the woodland from which white puffs of smoke divulged Pelham's position. Fortunately, the first enemy rounds fell short as was customary in getting the range. While the Yankees reloaded, Pelham skillfully withdrew his guns from the woods and returned to the Confederate lines where he met General Stuart.

"We stirred them up all right—and found a hornet's nest," Pelham grinned. "General McClellan has massed thirty powerful guns at the right end of his line. We could hold our own but I don't believe we have enough firepower to silence them so that General Jackson can mount an infantry assault."

"I must agree with you," "Jeb" said nodding, "I also found the Federal right too strong to attack."

When General Stuart relayed this information to General Jackson, the latter commented, "Too bad, too bad. We should have destroyed McClellan." Then as the two commanders reviewed the morning's engagement, "Stonewall" spoke warmly of Pelham. "He is a very remarkable young man," "Stonewall" observed, "This morning he commanded nearly all the artillery on the left wing of the army, and I have never seen more skillful handling of guns. It is really extraordinary to find such nerve and genius in a mere boy. With a Pelham on each flank I believe I could whip the world."

During the afternoon "Little Mac" shifted his attack to the center against "Old Pete" Longstreet's sturdy troops who steadfastly refused to budge. Unable to penetrate General Lee's left or center, General McClellan now ordered pompous General Ambrose Burnside to cross the lower Antietam and crush General Lee's right. But just as the bluecoats were ready to slice through the thin gray line and cut off the Confederate line of retreat, General A. P. Hill in his flaming red battle shirt arrived from Harper's Ferry with five brigades which he hurled against Burnside and drove him back to the banks of the Antietam.

Thus ended the bloodiest single day's fighting of the Civil War. Although General Lee did not proceed with his Northern invasion, he had managed to hold his own against an enemy force over twice as large under the command of a general who luckily had come into possession of a copy of the Confederate plans. A noted military analyst has stated: "From beginning to end of the campaign the Confederate commander's conduct was characterized by boldness, resolution, and quickness." And General Lee would have been the first to acknowledge that this same description aptly fitted his young artillery genius from Alabama.

Slipping through the net

CHAPTER VII

Riding Around McClellan's Army

WEDNESDAY'S FIGHTING at Antietam Creek left General Lee with only 27,000 battle effectives with which to face "Little Mac's" reinforced army of 75,000. Despite these odds, the Confederate commander audaciously remained in position the next day as though daring the Army of the Potomac to attack. Throughout the bright autumn day Pelham kept his guns unlimbered and ready for instant action. His crews, standing at arms, spoke in whispers and kept their eyes peeled on the endless rows of blue-uniformed figures partially hidden by the brilliantly-colored autumn leaves that adorned the distant fruit orchards.

Late in the afternoon Federal squads carrying white banners marched to the Confederate lines to request a truce in order to bury their dead. Otherwise there was no activity, and not a single shot disturbed the lulling fall breeze.

After dark, General Lee ordered his army to march to the Potomac and recross into Virginia. Unfortunately, a drizzling rain softened the roads over which the wagons groaned and horses skidded. Von Borcke's poor overburdened mount slipped five times throwing the bulky Prussian into the mud much to the amusement of the foot-soldiers. Pelham's batteries and the cavalry brought up the rear to ward off any attack. However, the enemy made no attempt to follow until the next day. By then Pelham's guns were in position on the Virginia shore from which they kept the enemy at bay with a heavy cannonade. In order to keep "Little Mac" off his back, General Lee ordered "Jeb" Stuart and Pelham to move up the south bank of the Potomac to Williamsport. Here they were to put on a convincing display of force to create the impression that the whole army was edging its way around the Federal army to invade Pennsylvania.

Within a few hours this diversionary force was splashing across the Potomac at Williamsport. On reaching the Maryland bank the graycoats encountered an enemy outpost which they charged and dispersed with a few shots. Then began a flurry of activity. General Stuart, always a master showman, divided his two cavalry brigades into smaller units which he sent northward along various paths to make the enemy believe a heavy movement was afoot. Pelham trotted along with his guns on the left flank.

The ruse worked. Before long, Federal columns were seen approaching. Cautious "Little Mac" was sending cavalry together with General Mansfield's Twelfth Corps to check General Lee's latest maneuver. Noting that the approaching bluecoats would pass close to his position, Pelham invited von Borcke to ride with him to a nearby peach orchard "where we can enjoy some delicious fruit while we scout the enemy."

Together they climbed a couple of inviting peach trees— Pelham insisting that his 250-pound comrade scale the larger one which could bear his weight without breaking and revealing their presence. Between bites on refreshing, juicy peaches, the two officers estimated the number of enemy troops that were rushing to head off the "Rebel invasion."

After four cavalry regiments had passed, Pelham called to von Borcke, "Stuff your pockets with peaches, Heros, and let's get out of here before the infantry divisions in the distance get here and strip the orchard."

"Goot idee," grunted the Prussian, and he scrambled down the branches which bent and creaked under his enormous load.

When Pelham reported the large forces that were converging on Williamsport, "Jeb" said, "Good, we'll keep them off balance by jabbing here and there and then recross the river tonight."

All afternoon the cavalry, vigorously supported by Pelham's guns, skirmished with the enemy who seemed reluctant to accept battle until reinforcements arrived. For Pelham it was a lark—peppering a Yankee unit in one sector, then limbering up and dashing to another where the action was repeated.

Most of the citizens of Williamsport were sufficiently frightened by the gunfire that they took refuge in their cellars. However, one adventurous teen-age girl became so fascinated with Pelham and his gunnery tactics that she insisted on remaining with a battery that was firing on an enemy regiment marching toward the town. Pelham finally persuaded her to retire to safety by first allowing her to pull the lanyard on one of his cannon. Thereupon the cannoneers set up a cheer and nicknamed her "The Girl Cannoneer of Williamsport."

Toward nightfall the heavy roll of drums announced the arrival of enemy reinforcements, and their pressure was soon felt by both Stuart and Pelham. General Stuart, seeing that nothing further was to be gained now that he had succeeded in luring a sizeable detachment away from the Army of the Potomac, rode up to the position where Pelham was duelling with a distant enemy battery and said, "Major, take your guns across the river at once and cover the cavalry's withdrawal."

Turning to his crew, Pelham shouted, "Limber! To the rear! Gallop!"

Back on the Virginia shore, Pelham drew up his guns in a line and began firing on the enemy positions behind the town. Some of the shells fell short and set buildings afire and soon the sky was illuminated by the eerie glare of shooting flames. Then as artillery shells arched back and forth over the river in a gunnery duel, General Stuart's horsemen forded the river to safety.

After throwing up a cavalry screen extending thirty miles from Williamsport to Harper's Ferry, General Stuart and Major Pelham established headquarters on the grounds of "The Bower", Colonel Adam Dandridge's spacious estate bordering the Opequon River near Martinsburg. Here for the next month "Jeb" Stuart and his staff enjoyed true hearty Southern hospitality amidst beautiful surroundings.

Colonel Dandridge's rambling three-story white frame mansion occupied the crest of a hill overlooking ten acres of rolling lawns populated by towering oaks. In this idyllic setting a hundred light-hearted officers and their aides pitched white tents and tethered their horses.

While General Stuart inspected his lines every morning, Pelham drilled his five batteries of Horse Artillery which now included twenty-two guns manned by over 600 veteran artillerists. Pelham was justifiably proud of his crews who had fought unflinchingly against great odds in battle after battle. But he would not let them rest on their laurels. He personally saw to it that they kept themselves fit and ready at all times.

As the boyish-looking commander of the Horse Artillery put his men through their daily paces, he would lay a friendly hand on a rammer's shoulder, or smilingly compliment a sweating sponger. When necessary, he could reprimand a cannoneer.

The Bower

But he never shouted or swore; he simply looked his man in the eye and told him how to correct his mistake. Pelham chuckled one day when he overheard Jean of the Napoleon Detachment tell a new gunner: "The Capitaine, he never raise hob with us, but when he look at you—you do wat he say."

Pelham and his fellow-officers looked forward to the late afternoons and evenings which they spent enjoying the pleasant attractions at "The Bower." Almost every day there was some special event such as a picnic, party, tea, musicale, boating and riding. These activities were made even pleasanter by the presence of Colonel Dandridge's two lovely daughters, Sallie and Serena, and a niece named Miss Lily. Pelham had met Sallie the year before when he was serving under General Joseph Johnston at Winchester. Then he had admired her sparkling brown eyes and copper-tinted wavy hair. Now he found that she also possessed a fascinating personality.

Moving fast to beat the competition, Pelham soon monopolized Miss Sallie's afternoons and evenings. He was her constant escort at the dances held in the great hall of the stately mansion; together they rowed by moonlight on the glistening Opequon; they held hands and exchanged tender glances in the singing circle around the fireplace; and on Sunday afternoons they rode along country trails in a captured yellow army wagon which Pelham borrowed from "Jeb", who jokingly inquired: "Don't you think that all this romance will spoil your love of fighting?"

"I doubt it," Pelham replied with a sheepish grin, "but I must confess that I won't be sorry when this war is over and I can settle down and raise a family."

"Amen to that," mused the great cavalry chief gravely as he thought of his own lovely wife and two children who prayed nightly for his safe return.

Just as everyone was settling down into a comfortable routine at "The Bower," General McClellan sent his cavalry under General Pleasanton across the Potomac on a scouting expedition. By the time a courier dashed up to the porch of "The Bower" with this news for General Stuart, the enemy cavalry had pierced "Jeb's" lines and pushed into the streets of Martinsburg only five miles away.

Gathering his aides and the Horse Artillery, General Stuart galloped off to rally his troopers and check the enemy's advance. On reaching the outskirts of Martinsburg, Pelham unlimbered a battery atop a hill where the guns could sweep the imposing lines of Federal cavalry. Pelham's guns raked the enemy who halted and re-formed to attack. But General Stuart meanwhile had rallied his troopers and now led them in a furious charge which drove General Pleasanton's horsemen back across the Potomac.

Upon returning to "The Bower," Heros von Borcke announced that he would shortly direct and star in a dramatic production entitled "The Operation." The evening of the play, all of the officers and young ladies crowded together on the stairs in the darkened hall. There they saw a white sheet stretched across the doorway. When the performance began all candles were extinguished save those behind the sheet which silhouetted the shadow of a groaning patient (von Borcke) lying on a sofa. His normally enormous mid-section appeared about twice its usual size due to the clothing and pillows Heros had stuffed beneath his flowing one-piece nightshirt. As the patient held his stomach and writhed in agony, he screamed: "Oh mein poor tummy! Vere ist ein doktor?"

Thereupon a doctor (Colonel Brien of the First Virginia Cavalry Regiment) arrived in a stovepipe hat carrying a medicine bag. Before looking at the patient, he leisurely removed his hat and swallow-tail coat and pulled off his gloves. Then he knelt beside the patient and examined von Borcke's tongue and felt his pulse. Finding nothing wrong with either of these, he thumped the moaning patient's swollen stomach. When Heros yelped, "Oh mein Gott, Doktor, don't keel me yet," the physician cupped his chin in his hand and in a pompous voice stated: "I think something is wrong with your stomach. What did you eat for dinner?"

"Nodding unusual," Heros muttered, "choost some wegetables, meat und deezert."

Rolling up his sleeves, the doctor said, "Well, they'll have to come out."

Then seemingly thrusting his hand into von Borcke's mouth, he pulled out a whole cabbage, followed by five ears of corn which were held up behind the screen for the laughing audience to see. The patient's shadow went down a little in the middle, but not enough to suit the doctor, who again inserted his hand. This time he extracted a whole leg of ham and two dozen oyster shells. Again the silhouette diminished in size, and the patient's moans grew fainter. Still unsatisfied, the diligent physician reached in and plucked out the dessert—an immense watermelon.

Completely healed, the "thin" patient now jumped up from his sick-bed and joined "Doc" in swigging cider from a whiskey flask. The act ended with the doctor and his ex-patient tipsily dancing around the hall arm-in-arm.

These gay and romantic affairs at the restful Bower were soon interrupted by the grim realities of war. Although the Army of Northern Virginia was regaining its strength rapidly in northwestern Virginia, General Lee was concerned lest General McClellan steal a march on him by quick-stepping his bluecoated legions southeastward through Fredericksburg and capture Richmond. Therefore, the Confederate commander directed General Stuart to scout the enemy. "Jeb" was to find out where the Federal army was encamped and what it was doing. In addition, General Lee wanted the cavalry chief to range northward into Pennsylvania and destroy the railroad bridge near Chambersburg over which supplies were being shipped to "Little Mac's" army.

This was just the type of assignment "Jeb" relished. As he carefully read his orders the cavalry chief envisioned the possibility of making another ride around McClellan's army. However, he kept this thought to himself as any leak to the enemy would endanger the expedition. Hence he merely sent orders to his able and dependable cavalry commanders, Wade Hampton, "Rooney Lee" and "Grumble" Jones to assemble three small divisions totalling 1,800 picked troopers, and have them meet at nearby Darkesville on Thursday, October 9. Pelham, puzzled by his veiled orders but happy at the prospect of some action, was to bring along four of his most reliable guns and sixty experienced gunners.

Heros von Borcke was unable to accompany the raiding party because he had worn out his mounts in hard riding around the countryside. Even sadder was General Jackson, who of course knew what Stuart's orders were. "Stonewall" told "Jeb" that he would gladly go as a cavalry private in order to participate in the mission.

To throw any enemy spies off the track, General Stuart staged a gala formal dance on Wednesday night at "The Bower" to which he invited guests from the surrounding area. Unable to get a date, von Borcke agreed to provide the entertainment by swathing his huge frame in a frilly, flowing evening gown which covered dainty lace undergarments that rustled in a wide circle around an immense hoopskirt. Coyly fluttering a colored fan in front of his face, this uproariously ridiculous-looking "belle" waltzed with Colonel Brien who was disguised as a tipsy, red-nosed Irishman attired in an "undertaker's suit."

Pelham and Sallie rocked with laughter as they watched this

hilarious pair perform their antics. Then after dancing several quadrilles themselves, the young couple strolled hand-in-hand down the grove to the bank of the Opequon. Knowing that he was leaving on a mysterious mission the next day, Pelham asked his charming companion: "Sallie, I may have to go away for a few days with General Stuart, and I'd like to ask a favor of you."

"Of course, John, what is it?" Sallie replied demurely, eager to be of service to the most talked about young soldier of the Confederacy.

"When I left Alabama," John said, "my mother gave me a small Bible to carry with me. While I'm gone I'd like you to keep it for me."

"I'd be honored to take care of it for you," Sallie responded.

Pelham then turned the conversation to his future plans following the war.

"When I was at West Point I used to think I'd like to spend about five years after graduation at a post on the Western frontier learning about army life and getting first-hand experience in roughing it. But I'm getting all that and more in General Lee's Army of Northern Virginia."

"What do you want to do instead?" Sallie inquired.

"After this is all over I think I'd like to settle down in Alabama with a nice wife and put my engineering training to use building badly needed railroads throughout the Confederacy."

At that moment a hearty voice burst forth in song on the porch of "The Bower." Hurrying up the path to see who it was, the romantic couple discovered it was none other than "Jeb" Stuart himself who was serenading the guests. In the center of the circle Sweeney strummed on his banjo while "Jeb" made sweeping gestures with his plumed hat as he bellowed his favorite tunes, "Sweet Evelina," "Oh Lord, Gals, One Friday,"

"Lorena," "Dixie," and of course, "Jine the Cavalry." What the colorful cavalry leader lacked in tonal quality he made up in volume and feeling which brought rounds of applause and calls for encores.

An hour past midnight the party broke up amidst fond farewells. All next day "Jeb's" 1,800 troopers and Pelham's four-gun battery of the Horse Artillery drifted into Darkesville from which point General Stuart led them into bivouac near Mc-Coy's Ford on the Potomac. After supper the expeditionary force assembled to hear their leader read a proclamation in which he said:

"Soldiers: You are about to engage in an enterprise which to insure success imperatively demands at your hands coolness, decision and bravery; implicit obedience to orders without question or griping, and the strictest order and soberness on the march and in bivouac. The destination and extent of this expedition had better be kept to myself than known to you. Suffice it to say, that with the hearty cooperation of officers and men, I have not a doubt of its success—a success which will reflect credit in the highest degree upon your arms."

That night as Pelham and Breathed made themselves as comfortable as possible on the frosty ground, Jim remarked, "I wonder where we'll be this time tomorrow night. I suspect we'll wreck the enemy's communications and rush back to rejoin General Lee."

"Maybe so," Pelham replied dubiously, "but if I know General Stuart he'll try to accomplish as much as possible with the large force of crack troopers at his disposal. He may even repeat his feat of a year ago near Richmond when you rode with him around General McClellan's army."

At daybreak the bugler sounded "Boots and Saddles," whereupon the column sliced through the fog and sloshed across the Potomac. General Wade Hampton's advance guard easily surrounded and overpowered the enemy cavalry patrol which

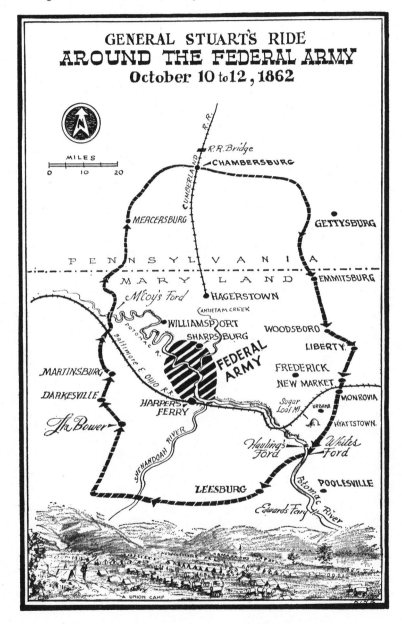

GENERAL STUART'S RIDE
AROUND THE FEDERAL ARMY
October 10 to 12, 1862

guarded the ford. Another party of graycoats then galloped to a nearby hill and seized a signal station which was manned by Federal wig-wag flag signallers.

From these prisoners General Stuart learned that only an hour earlier five Yankee regiments and two batteries had passed this point. "Jeb" whistled a sigh of relief at his good luck, for the one misfortune he did not want at this stage of the expedition was to encounter a sizeable enemy force which could tie him up long enough for "Little Mac" to rush reinforcements and trap the cream of Confederate cavalry north of the Potomac.

"Jeb" therefore lost no time in making a bee-line for Pennsylvania. General Hampton's 600-man cavalry division together with two guns of the Horse Artillery under Pelham's personal supervision led the four-mile long column. Colonel "Rooney" Lee's troopers fell in behind Hampton's, followed by the division commanded by "Grumble" Jones, a growling fighter who dressed his riders in homespun outfits. Two of Pelham's guns under Jim Breathed brought up the rear.

General Stuart had issued strict orders forbidding any plundering while the expeditionary force was in Maryland as he did not wish to do anything which might drive that state into the Union. Consequently, the cavalrymen maintained a fast pace and kept a sharp lookout for signs marking the Pennsylvania border. About 10 o'clock in the morning a cheer from Hampton's men and Pelham's advance gunners signalled their arrival in the rich Keystone state. Here General Stuart halted the column and had his commanders read the following order to their men:

"We are now in enemy country. Hold yourselves ready for attack or defense, and behave with no other thought than victory. If any man cannot abide cheerfully by the order and spirit of these instructions he will be returned to Virginia."

Now that the cavalry was in enemy territory, "Rooney" Lee's

troopers of the middle division broke ranks into parties of six which headed for the prosperous whitewashed Pennsylvania Dutch farmhouses where the farmers were threshing wheat. Passing themselves off as Northern cavalrymen, the officers demanded that the farmers surrender their powerful corn-fed Conestoga horses which would be ideal for pulling Pelham's heavy guns. "Jeb's" unshaven veterans winked at each other as the Dutchmen fumed about having to give everything to "Dot McClellan." Just before leaving, the leader of each raiding party would flabbergast the enraged farmer by giving him a Confederate receipt for his livestock.

After gathering all of the horses they could handle, the cavalrymen resumed their position in the column whose front and rear divisions had remained in formation to repel any enemy attack. When the moving column encountered buggies on the road, the troopers disconnected the horses and led them away from their disgruntled owners who were left sitting in a truly "horseless" carriage. Women, of course, were allowed to drive their vehicles through undisturbed.

At Mercersburg, a small village just inside the Pennsylvania border, Pelham wheeled two guns into the town square. Awed pedestrians quickly emptied the streets and closed their window shutters, fearful of what these strange bearded men might do. Their fears were groundless, for "Jeb's" troopers merely swarmed into the stores where they plunked down faded Confederate bills to pay for sorely needed shoes, clothes, and food.

Following this brief shopping spree, the graycoats—laden with packages—mounted their horses and trotted northward. Rain slowed the procession which reached the outskirts of Chambersburg after nightfall. Through the mist "Jeb" heard the ominous roll of drums. Uncertain whether this was simply a bluff of the townspeople to scare him away, or whether there actually were troops in the community of 7,000, General Stuart sent Wade Hampton ahead with a detachment to demand the town's surrender. At the same time Pelham unlimbered his two advance guns on a knoll from which he could sweep the town with artillery if the enemy resisted.

General Hampton, a courtly South Carolina cotton planter, conferred with a delegation of three frightened citizens who quickly agreed to surrender the town. While the terms were being drawn up, a squadron of gray troopers galloped into Chambersburg to seize the money in the bank. But they were too late—some alert bank official had removed the bundles of greenbacks from the vaults and hidden them.

That night General Stuart's expeditionary force encamped in the streets of Chambersburg which were lined with red-brick houses. Early the next morning "Grumble" Jones led his division to Conococheague Creek to destroy the Cumberland Valley Railroad bridge. However, on reaching their objective the men found that the trestle was constructed of iron which they could neither burn with their torches nor break with their axes.

Frustrated in their attempt to destroy the bridge, "Grumble's" troopers trotted back to the Federal supply depot in Chambersburg where they joined their comrades who were exchanging their tattered, rain-soaked clothing for clean, new overcoats, socks, underwear, sweaters and blue uniforms. After outfitting themselves the cavalrymen broke open a pile of crates and helped themselves to 5,000 shiny new rifles, pistols and swords.

Although "Jeb" had ordered the telegraph lines cut, a resourceful local operator had tapped out a message to Harrisburg notifying the governor that Confederate cavalry had captured Chambersburg. General Stuart knew that "Little Mac" would now rush infantry and cavalry to intercept him on his return to Virginia. Hence there was no time to tarry longer in this pleasant country town.

After the troopers and gunners had taken all of the supplies and arms they could carry, General Stuart ordered the rest burned. Then the buglers sounded assembly and the column turned west as though about to circle backward onto the route by which it had come. But as soon as the horsemen were out of sight of the town, General Stuart turned about and started east toward Gettysburg. He had decided to ride around Mc-Clellan's army.

Ideal weather favored "Jeb" for his ride around the Army of the Potomac. Damp roads settled the dust which ordinarily would have revealed the position of such a sizeable force of cavalry. And clear skies lessened the danger of being ambushed or of taking the wrong road. Actually, "Jeb" was not overly worried about losing his way for he had as his guide Captain B. S. White who had lived in Maryland before the war and knew every trail and landmark in this area.

At the head of the column rode three mounted sentinels or videttes whose duty was to act as the eyes of the column. Behind them cantered a cavalry squadron followed in turn by Pelham and his two forward guns. General Stuart rode near the center of the column to coordinate its movement. At frequent intervals he sent couriers to his commanders with orders to change mounts and keep the column well closed. All travelers encountered were seized and held to prevent "Little Mac" from learning the whereabouts of the raiders.

Before reaching Gettysburg, "Jeb" directed the advance guard to turn right as though heading for Hagerstown. After riding several miles in this direction to mislead the enemy, General Stuart veered southeast toward Emmitsburg. When the troopers crossed back into Maryland they stopped seizing horses. While in Pennsylvania they had collected 1,200 fresh, well-fed mounts which now trotted along beside "Rooney" Lee's cavalrymen who drew them along by the reins.

About sundown the head of the column reached the small village of Emmitsburg whose pro-Southern sympathizers were as startled as they were overjoyed to welcome General Stuart's 1,800 famed horsemen. However, one young lady who was visiting friends in this border town, became frightened when she stepped out onto the porch and saw squads of soldiers in their bright new captured blue coats they had appropriated in Chambersburg. Mistaking General Stuart's "bluecoats" for Federals, this terrified belle jumped on her horse and darted toward her home in the country. Fearing that she was riding to notify the enemy of General Stuart's presence, Pelham dug his spurs into his mount and pursued at a full gallop. On seeing that she was followed the young beauty urged her horse to greater speed but to no avail. Pelham, always a superb horseman, quickly overtook her and blushingly reassured her that he was a Confederate officer who would see that no harm befell her.

When Pelham and his blonde "captive" realized their mistaken judgments, they both enjoyed a good laugh and cantered back to town where the townspeople were plying their heroes with hot food and buttermilk.

General Stuart learned from the local authorities that less than an hour before his arrival four companies (about 140 troopers) of Rush's Philadelphia Lancers had passed through Emmitsburg on a scouting expedition in search of "Jeb's" elusive cavalry. With the enemy scouring the countryside for him, "Jeb" cut short his stay and ordered the column to push on. Again the flankers fanned out to protect each side of the column. Up front Pelham's guns set a fast pace for the quiet column to follow.

Through the darkness Pelham rode beside Captain Southall

who commanded the advance platoon. They were joined
shortly by General Stuart who galloped up and greeted them
cheerily.

"Boys," he said, "it looks like we have a full night's work
ahead of us. General McClellan is both embarrassed and infuriated by our second ride around his army. Right now he is
rushing cavalry to overtake us, and if that fails he has posted
General Stoneman's division of 5,000 men plus artillery to
guard the fords across the Potomac near Leesburg. Our chief
safety lies in our speed. Change horses often and run over anything that crosses your path. Major Pelham, keep your guns
moving and ready but don't fire them for we don't want to
disclose our position."

The cavalry chief had scarcely finished issuing these orders
and ridden back to hurry up the middle division when a young
Yankee courier dashed in front of the column. Pelham and
Southall quietly seized the intruder who turned out to be one of
Rush's Lancers. In his captive's dispatch pouch, Pelham found
orders which indicated that a strong enemy force occupied Frederick, and that General Alfred Pleasanton with 800 troopers
was at this very moment heading northward along the same
road down which General Stuart's column was advancing.
Pelham immediately sent this information to "Jeb" Stuart who
ordered the long line to move to the left so as to by-pass the
enemy cavalry. "Jeb" disliked having to side-step a fight, but
any engagement with the enemy at this stage would enable
"Little Mac" to concentrate enough forces to insure his
destruction.

"Jeb's" disappointment was soothed somewhat by an amus-
ing incident which occurred near Woodsboro. Here the head
of the column ran into a buggy driven by a Federal officer.
Annoyed at the troopers who barred his way, the irate Pennsyl-
vanian demanded that they step aside and let him pass. At

this moment "Jeb" rode up with an amused grin and drew rein.

"Are you in command of these men?" the bluecoat demanded, obviously unaware that he was addressing the famous Confederate cavalry leader.

"Yes, sir," responded General Stuart.

"Well get them out of my way. I'm a recruiting officer, and I'm on my way to fill my quota."

"Certainly," Jeb replied, and he whispered orders to an aide who climbed in beside the recruiting officer and took over the reins.

Before the dumbfounded Yankee could resist he was informed that he was General Stuart's prisoner and that from now on he would have to recruit Confederates to fight for "Little Mac."

Southward toward the Potomac clopped the horses, accompanied by the jingle of sabers and spurs. Hour after hour the horsemen rode on in silence. Although the night was clear the shadows soon became monotonous and many men dozed and snored in their saddles. Pelham, realizing his responsibility to keep awake at the head of the column to ward off a surprise attack, fought off fatigue by waving his hand in the cool night air to stimulate his blood circulation.

A little past midnight General Stuart rode by with several of his staff and informed Pelham that they were going to leave the column for a while to pay a short visit to the Cockeys in Urbana.

"Give them my regards—and those of Lieutenant Breathed and Major von Borcke," Pelham called out as the party rode off. While the gay cavalrymen serenaded the charming, hospitable Maryland belles, Pelham coaxed his guns through the muddy trails. When the column reached Monrovia, Pelham ordered the advance units to cut the telegraph wires and tear up the tracks of the Baltimore and Ohio Railroad.

At daybreak General Stuart and his staff rejoined the main body at Hyattstown. Since leaving Emmitsburg after supper, the cavalry had covered thirty-three miles. A combination of speed, darkness, and daring, skillful leadership plus a streak of good luck had enabled the five-mile column—now lengthened by the captured horses—to elude the enemy's far-flung net.

But the most dangerous leg of the expedition still lay ahead. Along the peaceful Potomac, only twelve miles distant, General McClellan had massed infantry, cavalry and artillery to teach these upstart Confederates "a lesson they will not soon forget."

If "Jeb" continued southward along his present route he would collide with General Stoneman's 5,000 Yankees at Edward's Ferry. If he turned right and headed for Hauling's Ford he would run straight into General Pleasanton's troopers. Either enemy force probably could delay Stuart long enough for Federal reinforcements to arrive in overwhelming numbers and capture the biggest prize of the war. "Jeb's" plight was further complicated by the presence on nearby Sugar Loaf Mountain of an enemy signal station which was flagging the raiders' position and route to Generals Pleasanton and Stoneman.

In this predicament "Jeb" confidently halted the column and conferred with Captain White. This capable guide described to Stuart a shallow crossing known as White's Ford located between heavily guarded Edward's Ferry and Hauling's Ford. General Stuart instantly ordered the column to continue toward Edward's Ferry for the benefit of prying Federal eyes atop Sugar Loaf Mountain. After proceeding six miles in this direction the column reached a forest which screened the troopers from observation. Here "Jeb" and Captain White wheeled sharply to the right and led the cavalrymen along an overgrown, unused trail which ran toward White's Ford.

Removing worm-eaten fence-rails as they advanced through

the woodland, "Jeb's" raiders soon emerged onto the road which led to Hauling's Ford where the Monocacy River flows into the Potomac. The column had just started down this road when the hoof-falls of enemy cavalry pounded louder and louder down the road. Soon General Pleasanton's troopers turned the bend and hove into view, whereupon "Jeb" charged the enemy column head-on. After firing a volley the bluecoats pulled back toward the Monocacy River where they intended to rally and thwart "Jeb's" attempt to crash through and cross the Potomac at Hauling's Ford.

But "Jeb" wasn't planning to use Hauling's Ford. His gray-coated troopers pursued the Yankee cavalry as far as a ridge which was located only two miles from White's Ford where General Stuart intended to make his dash across the river to Virginia soil. When Pelham galloped up with his two guns he saw at a glance the tactical importance of occupying this crest from which his cannon could hold off the enemy while Stuart's three cavalry divisions turned off to ford the Potomac. Holding up his hand to halt the gunners, Pelham ordered his crews to unlimber and open fire on the enemy.

The Federals assumed, as Stuart and Pelham hoped they would, that the Confederates were trying to blast their way to Hauling's Ford. General Pleasanton therefore brought up a battery to silence Pelham, but the Alabamian worked his guns so fast and accurately that the Yankee gunners had to change position three times to avoid being silenced themselves.

While Pelham blazed away at the enemy battery, Colonel "Rooney" Lee's cavalry division thundered toward the ridge where Pelham's guns were shaking the earth. Colonel Lee ordered a company of his sharpshooters to dismount and spread out on either side of Pelham's cannon and pepper the bluecoats massing down the road for an attack.

Colonel Lee then led the rest of his 600 troopers over a

farm road to White's Ford. Riding ahead to reconnoiter, "Rooney" spied a band of about 200 bluecoats entrenched on the rim of a quarry which commanded the approaches to the ford. To eliminate this threat so that the graycoats could cross unmolested, Colonel Lee sent a party under a white handkerchief of truce to demand that the enemy surrender or "be blown to hell."

After waiting fifteen minutes without receiving any reply, "Rooney" ordered his men to open fire on the quarry. But just as the dismounted Confederates advanced to storm the Federal position, they caught sight of the bluecoats high-tailing it down the bank of the river.

Now that the enemy had abandoned his strategic position beside White's Ford, Colonel Lee whisked his troopers across the river together with one of Pelham's guns which was ordered to protect the crossing from the opposite shore, 400 yards away. To keep the column moving, orders were issued that no horses be allowed to drink until they had reached the Virginia bank.

While the long column sped across the Potomac, Pelham continued to hold the bluecoats at bay for two hours. Using his favorite tactic, Pelham maintained a constant fire as he skillfully changed position to confuse the enemy and give him the impression that a large battery was in action.

In mid-morning "Jeb" rode up to Pelham and hurriedly informed him of a new threat.

"The Yankees are sending troops up the river against our left flank while General Pleasanton strikes us on the right," "Jeb" said calmly. "Most of our men have crossed the river, but the rear-guard isn't up yet, and I can't locate it. I want you to take your cannon down to the river and fire up and down the bank to hold off the bluecoats until the rear-guard arrives and crosses."

As Pelham replied, "Yes, General," the cavalry chief galloped off to hasten his column. Several minutes later when one of "Jeb's" aides dashed by in search of the rear-guard, Pelham waved his tall dark slouch hat and shouted, "We'll be here until you get back."

Following Stuart's orders, Pelham began to withdraw his gun to the river. He ordered his crew to move the gun a short distance, fire a few rounds, and then move nearer the river. This orderly retirement kept the enemy at arm's length thereby keeping a path open for the gray cavalry which continued to arrive and cross the river.

When he reached the Potomac, Pelham blasted Pleasanton's troopers and battery closing in on him from Hauling's Ford. Then he would turn his gun completely around and pour a withering fire on Stoneman's bluecoats from Edward's Ferry who were massing for an attack on his left. Back and forth Pelham played his gun against the converging enemy forces with such a devastating fire that the divided enemy was sure that a crack Confederate battery or two—and not a lone gun— was inflicting severe losses and thwarting a united assault.

About noon General Stuart's overdue rear-guard dashed into view on the ridge and rapidly galloped past Pelham's smoking guns into the Potomac. Shortly after the last of the column crossed, one of "Jeb's" couriers crossed from the Virginia side and handed Pelham a note which read: "Major Pelham, get your gun across the river—that's an order. Stuart."

Pelham obeyed without delay, but when he reached mid-stream the enemy opened a spiteful fire on the gray crews who had held them off all morning. When Pelham's comrades manning his other guns on the Virginia shore saw his predicament, they quickly silenced the Federal guns.

Now that they were back safely on Virginia soil, the raiders tallied up their gains and losses. The expeditionary force of 1,800 had covered 130 miles in three days through enemy territory crawling with bluecoats who dogged their trail all the way. They had seized 1,200 muscular horses, thirty Yankee politicians who could be exchanged for Confederate prisoners, and they had destroyed a quarter of a million dollars worth of the enemy's supplies and military property. All this was accomplished without the loss of a single Confederate. General Stuart's only loss consisted of two spare horses, "Skylark" and "Lady Margaret," who fell into enemy hands when "Jeb's" orderly got drunk and fell asleep while guarding them.

Following a sound and well-earned night's rest near Leesburg, Pelham accompanied his command back to "The Bower." Here he was given a hero's welcome by everyone from lovely Sallie Dandridge to curious Heros von Borcke who shook Pelham's hand almost to a pulp as he sputtered: "Velcome pack mine boy, und tell me all aboot yurr ride around der enemee."

And talk about it they did. Around the blazing hearth in the spacious living room of the Dandridge mansion the raiders related their many exciting adventures which occurred on this dramatic mission. General Stuart—partly because of his brotherly pride in Pelham and partly to embarrass the modest artillerist—insisted on describing the daring and skillful deeds of his blushing young chief of the Horse Artillery. The wide-eyed belles listened to these adventures with unbounded admiration for their hero. Their feelings were shared by a couple of English noblemen who were visiting "The Bower" to meet and interview the famed cavalry chief and his staff.

"Jeb" decided to celebrate his cavalry's homecoming with a ball on Wednesday evening, October 15. He sent invitations to everyone in the surrounding countryside to attend this gala affair.

With everybody in a jubilant mood to honor the successful raiders, the dance was a rollicking event. General Stuart was especially happy because his lovely wife, Flora, had come to visit him. Heros von Borcke and Colonel Brien added to the gaiety with their hilarious stunts. And John Pelham, attired in his full dress uniform, spent the evening hovering over Sallie Dandridge. During a lull in the dancing the couple strolled hand-in-hand beneath a harvest moon which illuminated the dewy lawn. Again they discussed their dreams of the future— when the war would be over and there would be no more partings.

But the very next morning John had to bid Sallie a hasty farewell when word was received that the enemy was marching toward "The Bower." Pelham hustled his guns forward to meet the invaders and rake their lines with percussion shells that spread explosive destruction among the bluecoats. However, the Yankees stubbornly pressed ahead until one of "Stonewall" Jackson's brigades came to General Stuart's assistance and drove the enemy back.

Then for two glorious weeks General Stuart's command relaxed amidst the autumnal splendor of "The Bower."

Defending the Battery

CHAPTER VIII

"The Incomparable Pelham"

GENERAL STUART'S troopers and Pelham's artillerists always remembered the October they spent at "The Bower" as the happiest month of the entire war. In fact, the graycoats fondly hoped that General McClellan would postpone any further campaigning until spring so that they might enjoy Colonel Dandridge's hospitality during the coming winter.

But "Little Mac"—stung by General Stuart's humiliating raid—was in no mood to oblige the cavalrymen and gunners comfortably ensconced on the banks of the Opequon. The end of October he ordered his 115,000-man army to cross the Potomac below Harper's Ferry and move east of the Blue Ridge Mountains to threaten General Lee's 70,000 veterans of the Army of Northern Virginia.

Uncertain whether the Union army was heading for Richmond or the Shenandoah Valley, General Lee kept "Stonewall" Jackson's Second Corps in the Valley and sent "Old Pete" Longstreet's First Corps over the mountains to Culpeper. With the two wings of his army separated by fifty miles, General Lee directed General Stuart and the Horse Artillery to form a protective shield strong enough to prevent the Yankees from driving between Jackson and Longstreet and then falling on each corps separately.

In compliance with orders, "Jeb" broke camp on Wednesday, October 29. After striking their tents and packing their trunks, Stuart's officers rode up the lanes through a driving rain to "The Bower" for their farewells. Pelham concealed his sadness at having to leave Sallie by taking her soft hands in his and lightly bantering.

"Don't worry, Sallie," he said with a smile. "We'll drive General McClellan out of Virginia and return to 'The Bower' before Christmas."

"That would be the nicest Christmas present we could have," Sallie said hopefully, cheered by the prospect.

At that moment the bugler sounded Assembly and the gray-coats formed in column of fours. As they rode off the troopers looked back and waved to their hospitable hosts.

While General Stuart led his horsemen through the Blue Ridge at Snicker's Gap, Pelham's guns rumbled further south and crossed at Ashby's Gap. Along the way farmers and their children plied Pelham and his men with food and invitations to spend the cold night in their homes. But with 5,000 enemy cavalry in the vicinity, Pelham politely explained that he had to push on to join General Stuart.

The cavalry and Horse Artillery again joined forces near Bloomfield east of the Blue Ridge. Here on the last day of October, "Jeb" learned that a force of Yankee cavalry was stretched across Snicker's Gap Turnpike at Mountsville Post Office only six miles away.

Within a few minutes after the bugler sounded "Boots and Saddles", the graycoats were galloping northward to meet the foe. Before reaching Mountsville, General Stuart sent the Ninth Virginia Cavalry Regiment along a trail which circled around to the rear of the blue-coated troopers whom "Jeb's" scouts quickly identified as three companies of Rhode Island cavalry.

At a prearranged signal—the firing of one of Pelham's guns —Stuart's divided regiments raised the Rebel Yell and charged the unsuspecting Yankees in front and rear. Startled by the headlong rush of the sword-brandishing graycoats, the Rhode Islanders hopped into their saddles and turned to flee. But before their mounts could gather speed they were overtaken and their riders cut down or captured. The handful who escaped were pursued five miles to Aldie where strong Federal reinforcements checked the thundering graycoats.

Angry at the heavy losses in the Rhode Island detachment, General Bayard, the Federal commander, determined to teach Stuart a lesson—a vow every previous opponent of "Jeb's" had made in vain. He ordered his artillerists to wheel their guns into battery and fire a barrage of percussion shells which exploded in the midst of Stuart's troopers causing severe damage to the horsemen and their mounts.

"Jeb" retaliated by bringing up the Horse Artillery which rushed into battery on a hill and opened fire with solid shot. Pelham's fire was so telling that General Bayard's gunners moved out of range to avoid direct hits.

While this action was booming, General Stuart re-formed his cavalry behind Pelham's guns for a frontal charge. But just as "Jeb" was in position to attack General Bayard's superior numbers, he received word from a scout that a long column of Federal cavalry was fast approaching from Leesburg. With the odds against him already high, "Jeb" decided not to risk being taken in flank by the enemy reinforcements while he was assailing Bayard in front. Reluctantly, he called off the attack and withdrew to Middleburg.

The next day Stuart and Pelham rode north to intercept the

Federal cavalry which had come to General Bayard's assistance at Aldie. This mounted force was under the command of General Pleasanton, who had allowed Stuart to slip through his net on the ride around McClellan's army. General Pleasanton was eager to avenge himself by blazing the way for "Little Mac's" army through the Blue Ridge at Ashby's Gap. Once in the Shenandoah Valley the Army of the Potomac could fall on "Stonewall" Jackson's Second Corps from the rear, and then recross to Culpeper and overwhelm the other half of General Lee's army under "Old Pete" Longstreet.

General Stuart collided with Pleasanton at the tiny village of Mountsville Post Office. The advance guards of both commands skirmished briskly in a feeling-out action. When the rival commanders determined each other's strength, they sparred for an opening. Late in the afternoon General Pleasanton caught one of "Jeb's" regiments off balance on a hill and drove the graycoats back to Pelham whose smoking guns spewed a storm of double canister which checked the enemy charge. With darkness approaching the opposing forces broke off the action and bivouacked for the night.

Next morning when the graycoats rolled out of their blankets they discovered that General Pleasanton had slipped around them during the night and joined an infantry brigade headed for Ashby's Gap. Without taking time to cook rations, the Confederates raced to overtake the bluecoats who had stolen a march on them. Four miles northwest of Mountsville Post Office General Stuart caught sight of the Federal cavalry followed by an infantry column, four abreast.

"Jeb" instantly ordered his men to head for the heights above the town of Union where they could block the enemy's advance. By the time Stuart's troopers reached Union and dismounted to take their position behind stone fences, Pleasanton's horsemen trotted into view and formed for the charge.

The first assault was repulsed by a shower of lead from "Jeb's" boys who lay hidden behind the stone wall until the bluecoats advanced to within fifty yards. Then they rose as one man and delivered a deadly volley which felled dozens of horses and riders. This musketry fire was supported by Pelham's guns, posted on a rise at the end of the line, which tore large holes in the enemy's ranks with a barrage of double canister.

Although he suffered heavy losses, General Pleasanton resolved to open a path through the Blue Ridge Mountains to "Stonewall's" rear. He decided the best way to accomplish this would be to sting Stuart and Pelham with a series of hit-and-run attacks which would gradually weaken and exhaust the graycoats. Then he would send the infantry brigade in for the kill.

Time after time Pleasanton's gallant troopers worked their way to General Stuart's lines and delivered a withering fire from their carbines. Each attack on the stone wall was co-ordinated with a flank jab at Pelham's battery. The Federal sharpshooters detailed to harass Pelham would approach the side of his battery, pick off a horse or two, and then gallop back to shelter where they reloaded. Pelham's anger rose as more and more of his indispensable draft horses slumped groaning to the ground.

When a well-aimed enemy percussion shell hit a caisson and exploded killing Private Johnny Phillips and Corporal Charley Costigan, Pelham's temper reached the breaking point. His blue eyes flashed and he sternly ordered the crew of his nearest howitzer to follow him along a concealed path to a hill that overlooked the field over which enemy sharpshooters repeatedly advanced to pepper his battery.

The next time the bluecoated squadron returned to pick off more horses and men of the Horse Artillery, Pelham waited until the column formed for the charge. Then he shouted, "Fire!" whereupon the cannoneer pulled the lanyard to spray a hail of canister in the midst of the startled enemy who had not seen Pelham move his gun to this new position. A number of Yankees were killed outright, and the remainder seemed stunned by this surprise blow which sandwiched them between Pelham's gun and Stuart's line.

Seeing their confusion, Pelham yelled, "Come on men, let's charge them!" Then waving his hat in one hand and a revolver in the other, he dashed ahead and within a few moments his little command had captured a number of prisoners, horses, and an enemy flag.

After suffering this setback, General Pleasanton stopped any further hit-and-run tactics against Pelham. However, he continued to apply increasing pressure on "Jeb's" flanks which caused the entire line to pull back a mile to Seaton's Hill. Here Pelham wheeled his six guns into battery on a hill which swept the field over which the Federals were advancing. He was still chagrined at the loss of his two men killed in the explosion earlier that day. Hence, when he espied a Yankee regiment moving toward his flank, he rolled up his sleeves and personally sighted the nearest cannon at the enemy color-bearer 800 yards distant. As he shouted, "Here's one for Johnny and Charley," the cannoneer pulled the lanyard which sent the perfectly aimed shell screaming toward the mark. When the shell exploded it cut down the color-bearer and spread destruction among the front-line troops.

Pelham's guns and Stuart's sharpshooters managed to hold off the bluecoats until dark when "Jeb" ordered a withdrawal to Upperville, a hamlet astride the turnpike at Ashby's Gap.

That night General Stuart wrote his official report to General Lee in which he stated:

Having to protect all avenues leading to my rear, my effective force
for fighting was much diminished; but the Stuart Horse Artillery under
the incomparable Pelham, supported by the cavalry sharpshooters, made
a gallant and obstinate resistance, maintaining their ground for the
greater part of the day.

General Stuart had just completed this report when he
heard suspicious rustling and breaking of cornstalks in a nearby cornfield. Quietly making his way to a stone fence behind
which Pelham was sleeping, he shook his brillant artillerist.
When Pelham opened his eyes and raised himself to a sitting
position, "Jeb" whispered, "The Yankees are moving into the
cornfield under cover of darkness in order to launch a surprise
attack at daybreak. I want you to take your guns as noiselessly
as possible to the hill above the cornfield and be ready to let
them have it full blast before they charge us."

"Yes, General, I'll rouse my crews and move the battery
within the hour."

When the faint November sun penetrated the darkness at
dawn the next day Pelham, from his position beside the guns
on the hill, noted strange movements in the cornfield. Before
long, masses of bluecoats stealthily crawled toward General
Stuart's line of dismounted troopers. But before they could rise
and charge, Pelham ordered his waiting gunners to open fire
with double canister. The first salvo nailed many would-be attackers to the ground, while the rest of the astonished Federals turned and dashed through the cornfield toward the other
end of Upperville. Here they rallied behind fresh infantry reinforcements.

General Pleasanton now advanced his infantry and cavalry
in a joint offensive which met stiff resistance from Confederate
muskets and cannon. However, General Stuart quickly realized
that his vastly outnumbered band could not continue to stand
its ground without being overpowered. His graycoats must

retire toward Ashby's Gap, while they made the pursuing Federals fight for every foot of ground.

"Jeb" sent orders for Pelham to cover the withdrawal by firing a curtain of lead at the enemy. Pelham obliged with a belching fire from all six cannon. After "Jeb's" troopers had pulled out of Upperville, Pelham limbered his fieldpieces and galloped to a new position where they unlimbered and again went into action against the pursuers.

Moving from one hill to another, the Horse Artillery repelled every enemy attempt to break through and assail Stuart's cavalry with infantry, artillery and cavalry. Irritated by the ability of Pelham's six guns—firing furiously and unerringly—to delay his advance, General Pleasanton detailed a crack squadron of sharpshooters from the Third Indiana Cavalry Regiment to take position behind a thick stone wall a couple of hundred yards from Pelham's battery. From this vantage the Hoosier marksmen began picking off Pelham's gunners and horses. Pelham struck back by raking the wall with double canister but the shells simply ricocheted.

Seeing that the Horse Artillery was in trouble, Heros von Borcke rode up with two cavalry squads and shouted, "If you vill sdop firing, Pelham, vee will charge der Yankees behind dot vall."

Pelham stopped firing and von Borcke led his troopers toward the wall. But the enemy fire was so murderous that von Borcke ordered his men to turn back after they had covered about half the distance to the stone fence. He told Pelham, "Vee can't take dot position mit dis few men. But vy don't you change to dot grapeshot und rip holes in ler vall?"

"Bully idea," Pelham exclaimed, and he gave the order, "Change to grape, men."

In less than a minute all six guns were blasting gaping holes in the wall, whereupon the Indiana riflemen scampered to the rear pursued by von Borcke's yelling troopers bent on revenge.

That night General Stuart's command encamped near Ashby's Gap. After posting his sentinels, "Jeb" called Colonel Tom Rosser and Major John Pelham to his tent.

"Gentlemen," "Jeb" began, "I am going to leave in a few minutes to cross the mountains to Millwood where I intend to confer with General Jackson about our next move. During my absence Colonel Rosser will command the cavalry. Major Pelham, I am counting on you to continue your splendid rearguard tactics which have kept General Pleasanton at a safe distance and enabled the troopers to make orderly withdrawals when necessary."

General Stuart shook hands with his two officers and then rode through Ashby's Gap which sliced between the towering Blue Ridge Mountains. As Tom and John watched their tireless chief disappear in the distance, the two ex-classmates fell to talking about their experiences together at West Point.

"John, did you ever think five years ago that you would be fighting along the Blue Ridge Mountains with a six-gun battery?"

"Never in my wildest dreams," John replied with a wry smile. "I figured on spending some time at a Western frontier post and then settling down as a civilian engineer in Alabama. Now I just hope we can beat McClellan before all of our fine men and boys are killed or maimed. It won't do us any good to win if all of our future leaders are wiped out."

"You're absolutely right," Tom agreed, "but I can't see how we can lose with leaders like Generals Lee, Jackson, Longstreet and Stuart. In fact, I'd be willing to bet we'll win by the end of the year."

On this hopeful note the two parted to catch a few winks before resuming the formidable task of tackling an enemy that was daily showing greater strength and skill. At daybreak

General Pleasanton renewed the attack. Applying pressure relentlessly all along the line he forced Rosser and Pelham to give ground and head for Manassas Gap where General Hampton's cavalry, which had been detached on another mission, was expected to rendezvous.

But shortly before sunset while Rosser's troopers were still separated from Hampton's, two Yankee regiments skillfully maneuvered to cut off and surround Pelham's guns which were in position on a hill together with a detachment of Colonel Jim Gordon's First North Carolinians.

Never before had Pelham been caught in such a tight spot. However, this danger served only to spur his determination to fight his way out of the ring of bluecoats now massing to capture the Horse Artillery and its renowned commander. When Jim Breathed dashed up to receive his orders, he found Pelham sitting calmly on his spirited black charger.

"Major," Breathed said breathlessly, "you certainly don't appear to be concerned about our desperate situation."

"Well," Pelham replied with a twinkle, "we're sure in for a tough fight, but we've never yet lost a cannon and I don't intend to now. Our boys will give a good account of themselves."

After instructing Breathed what to do, Pelham turned to his Napoleon Detachment which was lustily singing the "Marseillaise" while little Jean—his tousled jet black hair dangling over his forehead—aimed the guns at the crack New York cavalry regiment making its way up the hill.

Pelham cautioned the crew, "Load all of the guns with double canister and then hold your fire until I give the order."

While the Creoles executed this directive, Colonel Gordon's troopers dashed downhill to rout the enemy. But the charging mounts stumbled in a ditch on the slope throwing the riders to the ground. As the horsemen picked themselves up and tried

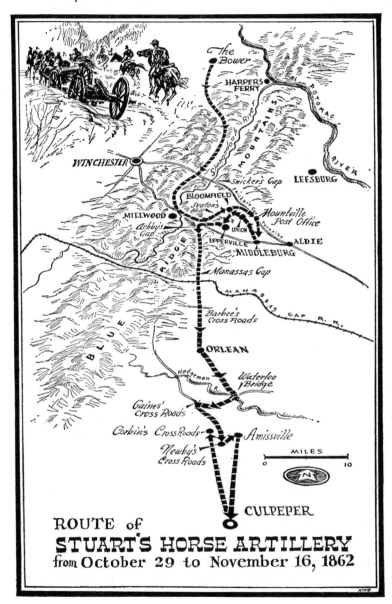

ROUTE of
STUART'S HORSE ARTILLERY
from October 29 to November 16, 1862

to raise their horses the bluecoats fired a heavy volley which forced the North Carolinians to scramble back up the hill where they rallied behind Pelham's guns. Colonel Gordon was furious at this mishap which prevented him from rolling back the enemy, but Pelham quietly reassured him.

"Never mind, Colonel," he said earnestly, "they won't run over us. We'll hold them off while you re-form for another charge." Then standing in his stirrups he shouted, "Fire!"

With a roar the six cannon belched their deadly fusillade which overturned Yankee troopers that had approached within a hundred yards of the Confederate line. Unable to advance in the face of this storm of flying shells, the bluecoats withdrew and straightened their lines for another assault. This time, however, the dismounted Federal sharpshooters spread out as they moved forward on foot to take advantage of the cover afforded by trees and boulders which covered the slope.

Pelham's Napoleon Detachment was pouring a steady fire on the bluecoats working their way up the hill, when suddenly another enemy regiment burst out of the woods in the rear of the battery and charged straight for the guns.

Seeing that he was about to be taken from behind, Pelham shouted, "Action rear!" whereupon his gunners wheeled two guns around to check the danger there. For half an hour Pelham's guns fired furiously in two directions at the same time— four concentrated their shot on the bluecoats in front while the other two blazed away at the force in back. During this fierce exchange a number of valiant Yankees struggled up the hill and attacked the cannoneers. Pelham drew his saber and came to the assistance of his gunners who were locked in hand-to-hand combat with a foe determined to seize the guns at any cost.

While the fight see-sawed back-and-forth, Colonel Tom Rosser arrived with his troopers. On seeing the dire peril of

Pelham and his crews, the graycoated horsemen drew their sabers, raised the curdling Rebel Yell, and charged the dismounted Federals. Within a few minutes they had cleared the slopes of bluecoats except for those who lay dead and wounded.

After dispersing the bluecoats, Tom Rosser joined Pelham beside the guns. "I see you still have six cannon," Rosser said with a look of pleasure as he finished counting them.

"Yes," Pelham grinned, "they gave us a rough time, and we owe a lot to you and your men for coming to our aid when we were so hard pressed."

Although the graycoats were tired, Pelham and Rosser ordered them to fall in and head for Barbee's Cross Roads where they were joined that night by General Hampton's troopers and General Stuart who had just returned from his conference with General Jackson.

During the freezing days which followed, "Jeb" led his column across the Rappahannock River at Waterloo Bridge and thence southwestward through Gaines' Cross Roads to Newby's Cross Roads. The Horse Artillery formed the rear-guard and kept General Pleasanton's pursuers at a respectful distance each leg of the snow-covered way.

General Stuart, in his official report to General Lee, described Pelham's tactics in this series of engagements which became known as the "Ten Days Battles" as follows: "His guns only retired from one position to assume another, and opened upon the enemy a fire so destructive that it threw their ranks into confusion and arrested their further progress."

When "Jeb's" scouts reported that General Pleasanton showed no signs of stirring from Corbin's Cross Roads, General Stuart decided to take the offensive and strike back at the foe who had become so aggressive. Accordingly, on Monday, November 10, the cavalry chief started north with cavalry, infantry and four guns of the Horse Artillery under Pelham.

"Jeb's" leading cavalry squadron struck Pleasanton's picket line on the snowy ground at Corbin's Cross Roads. The Yankee sentinels broke and fled to warn the main cavalry who in turn fell back before Stuart's furious onslaught. But just as "Jeb" prepared to deliver the finishing blow, enemy buglers blew the call to charge whereupon an unnoticed enemy brigade arrived from Amissville to assail Stuart's flank. Hopelessly outnumbered, "Jeb" had no alternative but to try to break off the fight and retire with as many men and guns as possible.

While "Jeb's" buglers sounded the retreat, Pelham, in his high top boots and snug gray overcoat, leaped from his horse and helped man the guns which alone stood between the horde of bluecoats and "Jeb's" retreating troopers and infantry. Before leaving the field of battle, "Jeb" paused to admire the calm, efficient manner in which Pelham covered the withdrawal. The cavalry chief later described this action as follows:

"Major Pelham exhibited a skill and courage which I have never seen surpassed. I was struck more than ever with that extraordinary coolness and mastery of the situation which more eminently characterized this youthful officer than any other artillerist who has attracted my attention. His eye for ground and ability to instantly size up a situation with the eye of a military genius, and his dispositions are always such in retiring as to render it impossible for the enemy to press us without being severely punished for his temerity."

CHAPTER IX

"It Is Glorious to See Such Courage in One So Young"

FOLLOWING THIS ceaseless fighting in the Ten Days Battles at the base of the Blue Ridge Mountains, Stuart and Pelham proceeded to Culpeper where General Lee had established his headquarters with General Longstreet's First Corps. Here the army enjoyed a week's rest while the Union army changed commanders. President Lincoln had become impatient with General McClellan's inability to defeat General Lee, and on November 7 he replaced "Little Mac" with General Ambrose E. Burnside, whose style of wearing side whiskers started the fashion of "sideburns."

Eager to please the Northern politicians, General Burnside decided to out-maneuver General Lee by quick-stepping his 125,000-man army down the Rappahannock River to Fredericksburg. From this historic town it was only a two-day forced march to Richmond, where, he told his commanders, they should plan to eat Christmas dinner.

Unfortunately for the new Federal commander, "Jeb" Stuart detected the Federal army moving from Warrenton toward Fredericksburg. On receiving this information, General Lee immediately dispatched "Old Pete" Longstreet to throw his

First Corps across Burnside's path until "Stonewall" Jackson could march his veterans from the Shenandoah Valley and join in a full-scale battle.

The middle of November General Burnside and his newly-organized three "Grand Divisions" arrived at Falmouth, a village bordering the northern bank of the Rappahannock. Pointing his field glasses across the river, the bewhiskered commander studied the town of Fredericksburg and the steep hills beyond. Neither he nor his staff could discern any Confederate force other than a small local garrison guarding the town. But Burnside would not permit his men to cross the river—400 feet wide at this point—until the pontoon train arrived. By the time it came, General Longstreet's 31,000 foot soldiers had slipped behind Fredericksburg and dug in on the slopes which commanded an unobstructed view of the river and the Federal army.

With "Old Pete" Longstreet's infantrymen barring the direct road to Richmond, General Burnside probed various points along the Rappahannock in hopes of finding a weak spot where he could cross and break through the Confederate defenses. But General Lee anticipated this move and met it by stretching General Stuart's cavalry along the river for a distance of fifty miles.

"Jeb" ordered Pelham to take the Horse Artillery eighteen miles below Fredericksburg to Port Royal where the Rappahannock begins to widen. Here General Burnside had brought up four gunboats manned by 500 sailors and equipped with 21 guns. General Lee felt that his adversary might attempt to transport his army across the river at Port Royal under cover of the gunboats' heavy firepower. When General Stuart reminded the commanding General of Pelham's skill in chasing away the Federal gunboat, U.S.S. Marblehead, on the Pamunkey River the year before, General Lee enthusiastically agreed that the Alabamian should be assigned to keep tabs on this enemy naval force.

Every day for ten days Pelham ordered his gunners to fire several rounds at the gunboats to force them to pull up anchor and keep moving. This tactic kept the fleet scattered and let the Federals know their movements were observed. However, General Lee soon became so suspicious of the heavy enemy activity on the shore opposite Port Royal that he sent one of "Stonewall" Jackson's recently-arrived divisions under General Daniel H. Hill to reinforce Pelham. Upon consulting together, Hill and Pelham agreed on a joint action to drive the fleet away from this sector.

On Friday, December 5, they put their plan into operation. General Hill ordered one of his own artillerists, Captain Bob Hardaway, to open fire on the gunboats with a breech-loading Whitworth gun at a distance of three miles. The gunboats replied feebly for a while, but when Hardaway's shells began splashing water onto the decks, the boats hoisted anchor and started downstream toward Chesapeake Bay.

Hardly had the vessels steamed out of Hardaway's range than they were greeted by two of Pelham's 3-inch Blakelys perched on a high bank overlooking the river. The opening salvo at a range of 300 yards sent two shells straight through the side of one of the warships. The infuriated Federal naval gunners replied with a storm of grape and canister which amputated the leg of one of Pelham's crew. This roused the gallant cannoneers of the Horse Artillery to increase their destructive rate of fire to a round every two minutes thereby causing the gunboats to scurry down the river to return no more.

During the bitterly cold week that followed this engagement at Port Royal, Pelham's men endeavored to keep warm by organizing snowball fights. Many from the Deep South had never before seen snow, and their discomfort was mixed

with curiosity at this new experience. Stuart and Pelham frequently concluded their inspection tours on these nippy days by
dropping off at "Gay Mont" the spacious homestead of John
Bernard. Here they warmed themselves by sipping tea around
the hearth. The host's admiring young daughter, Helen, noted
in her diary: "Major Pelham also pleased us extremely, a mere
youth, apparently, beardless and slender almost to a fault, but
quick and energetic in his movements and with an eagle eye
that shows his spirit." Mr. Bernard urged his distinguished
guests to spend the blustery nights at "Gay Mont", but General
Stuart declined with thanks, saying "it was unsoldierly to sleep
in a house."

Between drills and snowball fights, Pelham and his men
sympathetically helped the pitiful procession of women, children and old men whom General Lee had advised to evacuate
their homes in Fredericksburg to avoid being caught in the
withering cross-fire of the battle he expected to begin any day.
The long line included mothers carrying babies on their backs
and stoop shouldered men trudging along burdened with heavy
packs jammed with provisions and clothes. Pelham's boys cheerily transferred the children and packs to army wagons and carriages which transported them to the homes of relatives and
friends in the vicinity.

On the blustery Wednesday afternoon of December 10,
Private Chancellor, one of General Stuart's couriers, rode into
cavalry headquarters at Camp No-Camp below Fredericksburg
and extended an invitation to "Jeb" and his staff to attend a
dance at his home in Chancellorsville, six miles away. "Jeb"
did not feel that he could leave his post with the enemy growing more and more active, but he agreed to let his staff go if
they promised to return by morning.

Without taking time to cook supper, the young cavaliers
spruced up as smartly as they could without benefit of a bath

and clean clothing. When they were ready the dozen officers and musicians clambered onto Pelham's yellow ambulance wagon drawn by four spirited horses. Away they skidded over the slippery frozen roads, with Pelham holding the reins and von Borcke operating the brake. One of the passengers was a young Englishman, Captain Lew Phillips of the British Grenadiers, who was spending his leave from duty in Canada to observe General Lee's army in action.

On the other side of Fredericksburg the rear axle snapped off at the wheel while turning at full speed, and the occupants were thrown onto the icy ground. Picking themselves up they repaired the axle and proceeded at a slower gait to the red buildings at the crossroads known as Chancellorsville.

Dismounting from the wagon, the bruised party marched into the large brick Chancellor house. Inside, Private Chancellor introduced the officers to the young ladies who had come from the surrounding farms. Without delay Sam Sweeney and the musicians filled the main hall and living room with lively music, and couples began pairing off.

At midnight the dancers interrupted their waltzing to enjoy a luscious hot meal. Then the dancing resumed until about three in the morning when von Borcke stopped the music and thanked the Chancellors and their lovely hostesses for a delightful evening. He explained, however, that the officers must be back at Camp No-Camp by dawn.

When the weary dancers rolled into General Stuart's headquarters at daybreak, they were jarred by the roar of 65 enemy guns firing from the north bank of the Rappahannock. Although fog prevented clear observation of the Federals, General Lee was convinced that General Burnside was laying down a heavy artillery barrage to cover his engineers as they laid pontoon bridges across the river. Since he hoped that the mammoth Federal army would cross the river and dash itself

to pieces against the impregnable Confederate defenses, General Lee did not dispute the movement other than to send General Barksdale's Mississippi Brigade of crack marksmen to harass the pontoon layers.

By evening the Yankees had succeeded in completing five pontoon bridges over which General Burnside hustled a brigade of General Franklin's Left Grand Division. Next morning the rest of Franklin's troops crossed together with 220 guns and General Sumner's Right Grand Division.

Although General Lee's scouts reported this movement, a thick fog again hid the enemy's activities from direct observation. During the morning, long-range Federal guns on Stafford Heights hurled 5,000 shells at Confederates engaged in fortifying and strengthening their position on the hills behind Fredericksburg. General Lee ordered his artillerists to hold their fire in order to save their precious ammunition for the fierce battle he knew would soon begin.

Late in the morning patches of fog lifted so that ...

the graycoats could catch glimpses of burning buildings in the town and the masses of bluecoats who were marching and countermarching on the south side of the river. Early in the afternoon General Lee decided to inspect his lines and investigate a report from General Stuart that a large enemy force appeared to be concentrating for an attack against the Confederate right. Accompanied by "Stonewall" Jackson and Heros von Borcke, General Lee rode along the seven-mile ridge manned on the left by "Old Pete" Longstreet's First Corps and on the right by "Stonewall" Jackson's Second Corps. As the party passed each division, cheers went up from the shivering, stout-hearted veterans.

General Lee was warmed by the spirit of his men and the strong position they occupied. His Army of Northern Virginia numbered 78,000 infantry and 306 cannon, which, as one gunner put it, "can sweep the plain so that a chicken wouldn't stand a chance in that field when we open fire."

If General Burnside intended to crush the Army of Northern Virginia and march "On to Richmond," his troops would have to charge across the broad open plain between the river and General Lee's graycoats on the ridge. Meanwhile, the defenders, shielded by trenches and barricades, could mow down the bluecoats a regiment at a time.

When General Lee reached the extreme right of the line he dismounted behind a barn and motioned for "Stonewall" and von Borcke to accompany him to a ditch from which they could observe the enemy's activities. Through their field-glasses they observed Federal troops, covered supply wagons and artillery crossing the pontoon bridges and taking positions opposite General Jackson's front. After watching the enemy's preparations for several minutes, General Lee turned to General Jackson and whispered: "General, it appears that

General Burnside will launch his main attack against your position."

With fire in his eyes, "Stonewall" replied, "General Lee, I would prefer to seize the initiative and attack them first. We can surprise them in the early morning fog tomorrow and drive them back into the Rappahannock."

General Lee stared thoughtfully ahead for a minute, and then said, "No, General, we'll let General Burnside wear his troops out attacking our strong position. Then perhaps we can launch a counterattack as you suggest."

That night General Stuart's staff huddled around the campfire at Camp No-Camp headquarters. Though snow covered the ground and a raw wind whipped through the trees, the officers stayed up late discussing where and when General Burnside would strike. During the day "Jeb's" staff had reconnoitered the front and watched General Franklin's horde spread out on the plain only half a mile from "Stonewall's" line. Everyone expected that a heavy blow would fall the next day. The ground was too rough and slippery for large-scale cavalry action, but Pelham smilingly suggested that the Horse Artillery could represent the cavalry in the pending battle.

After the others turned in to get some sleep, Pelham and Captain Phillips stayed up to talk about the organization and tactics of British artillery. Then they chatted about the possibility of England entering the war on the side of the South. Phillips explained that his country had been set to recognize the Confederacy at the time of General Lee's Northern invasion in September, but changed its mind when the Army of Northern Virginia returned to Virginia following the Battle of Sharpsburg.

As the Alabamian and his English friend retired to catch some shut-eye, Captain Phillips handed Pelham a narrow red-and-blue striped ribbon. "Major," he said, "this is my good-luck necktie which bears my own regimental colors. I'd like you to wear it for luck tomorrow and afterward return it to me as a souvenir."

"Certainly," Pelham agreed, touched by this gesture of friendship, "I'll be honored to wear it as a band on my hat."

Before daybreak on Saturday, General Stuart's camp was astir with officers munching biscuits and frying their quarter-pound daily ration of bacon. Everything was blanketed by a thick fog through which it was impossible to see further than fifty yards in any direction.

After breakfast General Stuart and his staff rode to Prospect Hill where General Jackson was issuing orders while seated on a huge charger decorated with glittering ornaments. When Pelham caught sight of "Stonewall" he rubbed his eyes and quietly asked "Jeb," "General, are my eyes deceiving me, or do I see General Jackson dressed in a new full-dress uniform adorned with gold braid?"

"Your eyesight is perfect," "Jeb" laughed, "General Jackson has simply chosen this occasion to wear the uniform I gave him when we were at "The Bower." Now he really looks like the military genius he actually is."

While "Stonewall" conferred with "Jeb," the enemy sprang to life. Through the mist came the roll of drums and the blast of bugles. Although the Confederates could not see the blue-coats, they could tell from the loud persistent buzz that two powerful armies were about to clash.

Presently General Lee rode up and asked General Stuart to ride with him to the end of the line. The commanding General wished to determine whether the foe was taking advantage of the fog to move around General Jackson's right flank and attempt to roll up the line. Although General Franklin's Left Grand Division could be heard opposite the extreme right of "Stonewall's" front, General Lee and "Jeb" saw no evidence

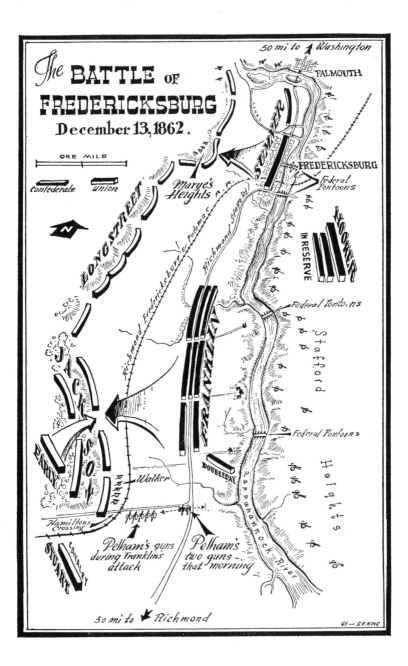

The BATTLE OF FREDERICKSBURG
December 13, 1862.

ONE MILE

confederate   union

50 mi to ↑ Washington
FALMOUTH

LONGSTREET

Marye's Heights

FREDERICKSBURG

Federal Pontoons

Richmond Fredericksburg & Potomac

Richmond Stage Rd.

HOOKER
IN RESERVE

Federal Pontoons

Stafford

FRANKLIN

JACKSON

EARLY

DOUBLEDAY

Federal Pontoons

Heights

Walker

Hamilton's Crossing

STUART
CAVALRY

Pelham's guns
during Franklins
attack

Pelham's
two guns
that morning

Rappahannock River

50 mi to ◀ Richmond

66 — S.E.KING

that any Federals were on General Jackson's flank. To prevent such a move, General Lee told his cavalry chief, "General, place Pelham and the Horse Artillery where they can break up any enemy demonstration against our right flank."

Before 10 o'clock the fog began to lift, whereupon General Lee directed General Longstreet to test the range of his artillery. The moment "Old Pete's" guns on Marye's Heights blazed away, General Burnside ordered his artillerists on Stafford Heights to reply. General Franklin took advantage of this artillery umbrella to advance his 55,000 bluecoats against the Confederate right.

As Heros von Borcke viewed the seemingly endless Yankee lines move forward—their banners flying and bands playing as though on parade—he turned to "Stonewall" and asked worriedly, "General, do you theenk ve vill be able to sdop all dot enemee?"

"Major," Jackson replied brusquely, "my men have never failed to defend a position. I am glad the Yankees are coming. If they get too close we'll drive them back with the bayonet."

"Stonewall" then calmly reached into his dispatch case and pulled out pencil and pad on which he wrote the following note to "Jeb" Stuart: "General, order Major Pelham to open fire against the advancing enemy."

"Jeb" passed this order to Pelham, who asked excitedly, "General, I would like to have permission to take two guns half a mile along a hidden path to a gully perpendicular to the Richmond Stage Road. Here I can pour an enfilading fire on the flank of Franklin's troops and knock them down like ninepins."

General Stuart stroked his bushy red beard a moment while considering Pelham's audacious proposal. Sending two guns to stop three regular Federal divisions unquestionably seemed foolhardy. The enemy most surely would quickly overpower this tiny island of resistance and kill or capture Pelham and his gunners.

But although the rules of warfare all opposed Pelham's scheme, General Stuart placed such confidence in his young artillerist's judgement, that he replied, "Go ahead, Major, but be careful to withdraw in plenty of time."

Grinning confidently, Pelham saluted and rode off with a Blakely gun and twelve-pounder Napoleon which he had captured near Richmond during the summer. The Napoleon Detachment trotted along to man the pieces.

Pelham managed to get his guns into position without being detected. Without delay the Creoles loaded the cannon with solid shot and aimed them so as to enfiade the Yankee front line only 500 yards away. Pelham, astride his frothing charger, waited until the solid blue row marched exactly into his line of fire. Then, with his red-and-blue tie flying in the breeze, he rose in his stirrups and shouted, "Fire!"

Startled by this flank fire, the enemy halted, and many infantrymen hugged the ground to escape the next salvo. While Pelham continued to rake General Franklin's divisions with a devastating fire that toppled the blue ranks like rows of falling dominoes, the Federal commanders ordered their batteries to wheel around and silence Pelham whom they believed must have unleashed at least an entire battery on their flank. Ere long, sixteen Yankee guns were raining shot and shell on Pelham's two guns.

For a full hour Pelham exchanged a raging fire with the enemy in a violent duel which filled the air with whining missiles that churned the frozen earth and bushes into dust and flying debris. Through it all Pelham, flushed with excitement at the sight of his two guns stalling the advance of Franklin's Left Grand Division, resolutely directed the operation of his guns. Above the din he shouted rhythmically over and over again, "Load! Ram! Fire! Swab!"

Whenever enemy shells whizzed close to the standing crews, Pelham barked, "Drop to the ground for half a moment after you fire." And when it seemed that the enemy guns finally got the exact range, he gave the order, "Shift position, men. Move the guns further up along the hedge."

Throughout the roaring confusion, Pelham continually observed the effect of his fire on the enemy, correcting the aim when necessary. "A little lower, Lieutenant, you're overshooting the battery," he directed, whereupon the next shot from the Blakely shattered the axle of an enemy fieldpiece. Lithe little Jean acted as cheerleader in celebrating this hit which toppled the Federal gun to the ground. But the enemy retaliated with deadly vengeance by exploding a shell squarely on the Blakely. One glance told Pelham that the overturned gun was out of commission. Even worse, Jean was stretched out on the ground hemorrhaging from a shell fragment which ripped open his chest.

Pelham instantly jumped off his horse and ordered the crew to move the disabled Blakely out of the way, while the other crew redoubled the Napoleon's fire. This done, he knelt beside Jean and tried to staunch the flow of blood which was spurting from his wound.

"It hurts some, mon Capitaine," groaned the plucky Creole gunner.

"I know," Pelham said comfortingly, "but you are a brave boy, and we will take care of you. I'll have Dominic and Paoli (two of Jean's fellow-cannoneers) carry you back to a surgeon as soon as we stop the bleeding and get your wound bandaged."

At that moment, giant Heros von Borcke rode up and reported to Pelham that General Stuart "preesents his compleements und says to tell you to come back to General Jackson's line ven you theenk best."

"Thanks, Major," Pelham replied, "but you can tell General Stuart I will continue to hold my ground as long as I have ammunition. Meanwhile, we're taking a heavy toll of enemy men and guns."

Not only did Pelham maintain his position, but his rapid, shifting fire completely halted the enemy's advance. General Franklin, impatient to move forward and assail General Jackson, reinforced the fire of four of his own batteries on Pelham with the firepower of long-range guns on Stafford Heights.

All along the Confederate right admiring eyes watched unbelievingly as Pelham with his single Napoleon dueled with a hundred guns and checked the advance of 16,000 bluecoated infantry. General Lee, observing this spectacle through his field-glasses, turned to an aide and exclaimed, "It is glorious to see such courage in one so young."

Meanwhile, General Stuart grew increasingly anxious lest the angry enemy turn its full force on the brilliant artillerist whom he loved as a brother. "Jeb" sent another message to Pelham requesting him to retire. But despite the loss of several more gunners, Pelham insisted on fighting until his ammunition gave out. Then and only then did he heed General Stuart's plea to "stop firing and withdraw your gun, you crazy gallant Pelham."

Coolly employing his flawless sense of distance and position, Pelham directed the withdrawal of his death-dealing Napoleon to the field bordering General Jackson's right. No sooner had he unlimbered his serviceable Napoleon than he found to his delight that General Jackson had rushed 14 guns for him to command. Knowing that the enemy was about to attack his front, "Stonewall" posted 14 rifle and Napoleon guns with Colonel Walker on the ridge to fire directly into the advancing bluecoats while Pelham raked their flank with a murderous crossfire.

Before moving his infantry forward, General Franklin ordered his batteries to soften up the Confederate line with a thunderous cannonade which lasted an hour. During this violent barrage, General Jackson forbade his troops and guns to reply. But when three lines of bluecoats—each three miles long with bayonets sparkling in the noonday sun—pushed forward to within a short distance of the ridge, "Stonewall" ordered Walker and Pelham to open fire in unison. The first salvo tore wide holes in the first line while the second barrage felled so many bluecoats that the three lines moved back to the Richmond Stage Road to regroup.

When General Franklin's troops again pressed forward toward General Jackson's line, their attack was coordinated with a fierce onslaught by General Sumner's Right Grand Division against "Old Pete" Longstreet's impregnable position on Marye's Heights. Walker and Pelham again peppered Franklin's shock troops with a deafening fusillade that rocked the front line which hesitated a moment as if deciding whether to retreat or advance. Suddenly the color-bearers dashed forward and the foot-soldiers followed. Through the withering fire of Walker's and Pelham's fast-firing batteries, the dauntless Yankees pushed ahead. In the middle of "Stonewall's" line they found an undefended swampy gap through which they funneled.

With the enemy fanning out behind General Jackson's front line, Pelham and Walker ceased firing until General Early brought up his reserve division and savagely counterattacked. Then as the bluecoats fled back through the gap they had recently penetrated, Pelham's fourteen guns sprayed them with canister.

By mid-afternoon General Jackson's front was restored and

Franklin's troops driven back to their starting position. "Stonewall" now proceeded to organize a full-scale counteroffensive aimed at driving the Left Grand Division into the Rappahannock. Pelham and Stuart advanced and fired on the weary Yankees, but the graycoats soon turned back when the enemy opened a merciless fire on them with long-range artillery across the river.

Meanwhile, wave after wave of General Sumner's infantry courageously charged the Confederate left only to litter the field with dead and wounded. The bluecoats had to charge uphill across open ground in the face of heavy artillery and musket fire delivered by graycoats lined up six deep behind the stone wall at the foot of Marye's Heights.

After repeated piecemeal assaults had been repulsed with heavy losses to the attackers, the Federal commanders implored General Burnside to halt this wholesale murder. But the bewhiskered commander angrily shouted, "That height must be carried by evening." But by twilight, General Burnside's army had lost 12,500 brave men without denting "Old Pete" Longstreet's line.

The Confederate high command fully expected General Burnside to renew the attack on Sunday. To protect his front against another breakthrough, General Jackson placed troops across the gap Franklin's troops had pierced. And to guard his right flank, "Stonewall" ordered Pelham to construct an earthen fort for the protection of his battery.

Before undertaking this task, which he knew would take all night, Pelham stopped at the surgeon's tent where Jean had been taken for treatment. The diminutive Creole's chest had been treated and bandaged, but the lad was writhing in pain. However, his eyes brightened as Pelham gripped his hand and said, "Bear it like the brave soldier you are."

"I try, mon Capitaine," Jean replied feebly, "but I'm afraid

Jean weel fight no more. I want you, Capitaine, to tell my papa and mama how I fight my best for you."

"That I will, for you have always fought bravely and to me you are a hero."

At these words Jean smiled faintly and peacefully closed his eyes for the last time.

Early Sunday morning Generals Jackson and Stuart inspected Pelham's battery which now was well protected by earthworks. "Good, good," "Stonewall" muttered approvingly at the fine overnight job Pelham and his men had done. Almost as an afterthought, he turned to "Jeb" and said seriously, "General Stuart, if you have another Pelham, I would like to have him."

"Unfortunately, there's only one Pelham, and I intend keeping him," "Jeb" rejoined emphatically, "but you may borrow him anytime you need him."

When General Burnside finally bowed to the casualty lists and desisted from further bloodshed, the two armies settled down for a period of rest and recuperation. Around Confederate campfires the chief topic of conversation was "the gallant Pelham" as General Lee described the artillerist in his official report of the Battle of Fredericksburg. This was the only report General Lee wrote during the war in which he mentioned by name the heroism of anyone below the rank of General.

Others joined in expressing their respect for the modest Alabamian. A cannoneer in the Horse Artillery proudly claimed that "no one made so much of a fight and so much of a name in so short a time as Major Pelham." A fellow-officer stated without reservation that Pelham "is the bravest human being I ever saw in my life." His fame became international when the London Times commented, "No one of an equal age in either army has won an equal reputation."

Everyone confidently predicted that John Pelham would be a Brigadier-General before another year passed.

His last battle

CHAPTER X

"He Is Irreplaceable"

AFTER THE GORY one-day Battle of Fredericksburg, General Lee decided to keep his army in its strong position on the ridge behind the town where he could maintain an eye on General Burnside's battered army encamped at Falmouth across the Rappahannock. Pelham promptly set about supervising the construction of comfortable winter quarters for his men. With considerable ingenuity they erected log huts equipped with fireplaces and chimneys.

General Stuart insisted that Pelham pitch his canvas shelter near the huge headquarters tent of the cavalry chief at Camp No-Camp. For added convenience Pelham installed a wooden floor and fireplace. Pelham's new tent-mate—now that Captain Jim Breathed had been transferred to Fitz Lee's command—was Major John Esten Cooke, a young Virginian who was an aide to General Stuart.

Before the war Major Cooke had graduated from Harvard to become one of the country's most popular novelists. Even now he devoted his spare time to writing a biography of "Stonewall" Jackson. Pelham and Cooke found that they had a number of common interests, and they spent many enjoyable evenings reading and discussing a variety of subjects. After supper the two tent-mates frequently joined the throng which congregated in the large log chapel to worship. General Jackson, a devout Presbyterian, often attended these meetings and led the prayers.

General Stuart's staff spent the week before Christmas preparing a gala holiday celebration. While Pelham and Cooke scoured the neighboring farms for Yuletide foods, von Borcke planned the entertainment. Although the weather was bitterly cold, a warm time was had by all in General Stuart's tent, where caroling, roast turkey, and von Borcke's rendition of Dickens' "Christmas Carol" set the holiday mood.

On Christmas night General Stuart announced that the next day he was taking 1,800 troopers together with Major Pelham and four guns of the Horse Artillery on a raid against the enemy's supply line to Washington. For almost a week this expeditionary force ranged behind the Federal army. "Jeb's" grayjackets would feint as if about to strike one place only to attack an unsuspecting unit elsewhere. When the enemy prepared to trap him, "Jeb" would outfox his adversary by having his men build endless campfires at night to make his force appear much larger than it actually was, and the bluecoats would fade away. Pelham helped too, by firing his guns so furiously that two of them exhausted their ammunition the second day out and had to be sent back to Fredericksburg.

Knowing that General Burnside would expect him to return to camp by the shortest route, "Jeb" led his men to Burke's Station within ten miles of Washington. Here he captured the telegraph station and sent a message to Quartermaster-General Meigs of the U.S. Army complaining that the Northern mules he had seized weren't healthy enough to pull the captured wagons loaded with supplies.

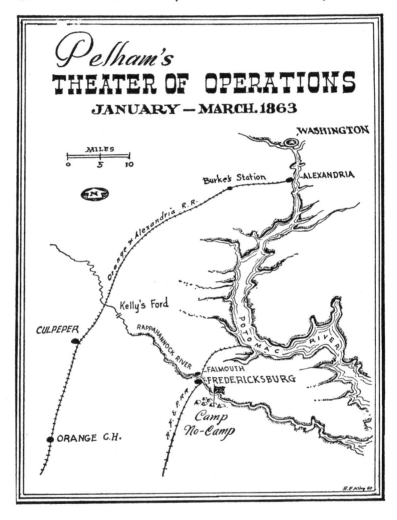

Pelham's
THEATER OF OPERATIONS
JANUARY — MARCH. 1863

Then before the panic-stricken bluecoats realized that they had been invaded by a cavalry force numbering less than 2,000, General Stuart circled westward around Burnside's army and rejoined General Lee at Fredericksburg on New Year's Day, 1863. His mission had netted twenty wagons, 200 prisoners, 200 horses and 100 rifles.

This cavalry raid, while not as adventurous and momentous as the rides around "Little Mac's" army, nevertheless caused alarm in Washington and kept General Burnside on the defensive. General Lee complimented the raiders for "striking a blow wherever the opportunity offered." And General Stuart with his customary pride reported, "Major John Pelham with his horse artillery performed gallant and exceedingly difficult service during the expedition."

In January the weather turned even worse than it had been during December. Heavy snows and sleet covered the ground, nights were foggy, and biting winds added to the army's discomfort. Late in January the snows melted and turned the earth into a sea of mud. General Burnside chose this time to seek revenge for his costly and humiliating defeat in December. He roused his troops and marched them a few miles up the Rappahannock which he intended to cross and fall on General Lee's flank. But after watching his troops and guns sink in the treacherous mud, the Federal commander cancelled his orders and the "browncoats" plodded back to camp where they learned that President Lincoln had replaced General Burnside with General "Fightin' Joe" Hooker.

For the remainder of the winter the rival camps enjoyed comparative peace as the two armies rested and gathered strength for the coming campaign. Pelham kept his guns ready and his crews alert for any enemy activity, for he knew that both "Stonewall" Jackson and "Jeb" Stuart were depending on him to repel any surprise thrust the Yankees might launch.

However, the Federals were interested more in trading than in fighting, and when officers weren't looking they would call over, "Hey Johnny Reb, we're sending tobacco and coffee over on a tiny raft. Send us back a deck of playing cards."

Pelham spent considerable time seeing that the horses used to pull his guns were well cared for. Many were suffering from what "Jeb" called the "greased heel and sore tongue" disease which resulted from strenuous campaigning and lack of feed.

On long winter evenings Pelham met with his fellow officers in General Stuart's tent where they whiled away the hours telling stories and singing. During one such session an aide of Stuart's asked Pelham why he hadn't been promoted for his outstanding performance at Fredericksburg.

"Yes, you certainly deserve a colonelcy if anyone does," Captain Blackford, "Jeb's" able engineer, emphatically declared.

"Oh, I probably look too young to be a colonel," Pelham replied in embarrassment. "Besides," he added, "I don't really want any promotion which would take me away from General Stuart."

But boyish looking or not, "Jeb" was determined that Pelham receive the promotion he had so justly earned. In a letter to the Government the cavalry chief wrote:

"The position which Major Pelham holds is one of great responsibility, and it should have corresponding rank. I will add that the coolness, courage, ability and judgment which Pelham has shown on many battlefields have earned him a promotion. So far as service goes he has long since won a colonelcy at the hands of his country. Though remarkably youthful in appearance, there are Generals as young with less claim for that distinction, and no veteran in age has ever shown more coolness and better judgment in the sphere of his duty."

To these sentiments General Lee added, "No one deserves promotion more than Major Pelham."

Fortunately, John Pelham was less interested in his rank than he was in engaging in some activity. Consequently, he eagerly accepted General Stuart's invitation to accompany Heros von Borcke and Lieutenant Channing Price on an inspection trip to Culpeper, a town thirty-five miles west of Fredericksburg.

Early Tuesday morning, February 17, the trio bundled up in their warmest clothes and bade good-bye to their comrades at Camp No-Camp. A driving snow slowed their progress, and by nightfall they were still ten miles from Culpeper. With snow piling up in drifts which impeded the horses, Pelham suggested that they stop overnight at the nearest farmhouse.

Soon the threesome—looking like mounted snowmen—ploughed along the forest trail into a clearing where they espied a lone farmhouse. Making their way to the porch the weary troopers saw a sign beside the door which read: "Madden-Free Negro." Pelham dismounted and knocked at the door which was then opened a crack by the colored owner who was obviously alarmed by the appearance of three strange callers in a blizzard. Glancing beyond Madden, Pelham caught sight of an inviting wood fire blazing in the fireplace.

"Madden," Pelham said as he clapped the snow off his gloves, "we are Confederate officers in search of a night's shelter from this storm. We'll pay you well if we can quarter here."

But the free Negro (who had been granted his freedom by his former master) was suspicious. After carefully eyeing the threesome, he nervously snapped, "I ain't gonna have nothin' to do with stragglers," and he slammed the door. The young artillerist strode back to his companions who were all for pushing on to Culpeper.

"No," Pelham dissented shaking his head emphatically, "it's dark and we could easily lose our way in the snow. Let me try a ruse which I think will change Madden's mind. You fellows just follow me."

"Go ahead, mine poy," chirped von Borcke as he dismounted, "vee'd rather sleep here dan fight der snows all night."

Remounting the porch steps, Pelham knocked and then pounded at the door until the frightened owner unlatched and opened it.

"Madden," Pelham barked sternly, "you must realize that we are your friends." Then pointing to von Borcke he said, "The tall officer with the beard there is General Lee and the other gentleman is the French Ambassador. I am General Lee's aide. We are on an important mission. Unless we can stay here tonight General Lee undoubtedly will order his artillery to shell your house when the gunners pass through here tomorrow."

Pelham spoke so convincingly that Madden muttered his apologies about thinking they were stragglers, and he cordially invited the distinguished guests inside. Eager to retrieve himself in the eyes of "General Lee", Madden dried his guests' clothes and served them a steaming supper.

When Pelham insisted on paying his host in the morning he tried to explain who the lodgers really were, but the confused Negro clung to the belief that von Borcke must be General Lee because he was so distinguished looking.

About noon the trio reached Culpeper where General Stuart later joined them for an inspection of General Hampton's and General Fitz Lee's cavalry units which were patrolling the Rappahannock. That evening the officers thawed out in Culpeper's Virginia Hotel where Fitz Lee's troopers presented a minstrel which of course included a skit about Madden's house —where "General Lee" slept overnight.

After the ministrel Pelham asked General Stuart to introduce him to a vivacious blue-eyed brunette he had seen in the audience.

"She reminds me so much of my sister, Betty," Pelham explained.

"Yes, of course," "Jeb" joshed, "every beauty reminds you of some relative or other. But come on and I'll introduce you to this Virginia belle whose name is Miss Bessie Shackelford."

Pelham fast discovered that Bessie possessed wit and intelligence in addition to her striking beauty. Knowing that he and von Borcke were to remain in Culpeper while General Stuart rode to Richmond on the morrow, Pelham asked Bessie's permission to call on her.

"Certainly, Major," she replied with a gracious smile, "we live just across the street, and you and Major von Borcke will be welcome any time."

Early the next morning Pelham and von Borcke were energetically engaged in laying a makeshift plank walk from the Virginia Hotel to Judge Shackelford's spacious home. Pelham had decided to throw this span across Main Street in order to avoid tracking mud into the house of his fair hostess.

When the narrow boardwalk was completed, Pelham and von Borcke crossed on it and spent the day in delightful entertainment. Bessie and her four sisters joined the officers in singing around the piano, playing charades, and discussing lively topics. In his inimitable bungling style, von Borcke described Pelham's deeds. Bessie was enthralled by these tales, but she simply couldn't believe, as she said, that this gentle, soft-spoken Alabamian "could ever order anybody to be killed. There wasn't a single line of hardness in his boyish face."

During the next two weeks Pelham and von Borcke crossed and re-crossed their plank walk to Shackelfords. Then early in March, "Jeb" ordered them to return to Camp No-Camp. Here Pelham promptly proceeded to whip his batteries into peak form for the heavy fighting which loomed ahead.

One day when it was too rainy to drill, Pelham visited his seventeen-year-old brother, Sam, who was stationed in a nearby camp. The brothers chatted all afternoon about the news from home and their plans for the future. As John was about to leave, Sam presented him with a twelve-pound cannon ball which John promised to deliver to the Yankees at close range.

On returning to his camp, Pelham found General Stuart waiting with a package for him. "Jeb" insisted that Pelham unwrap it then and there. Suspecting a joke, the young artillerist carefully untied the cord and gingerly removed the scented wrapping paper. But his suspecting eyes lit up and his mouth watered when he opened the box and found it chock full of taffy.

"Have some, General," he said offering the box to "Jeb."

"Thanks, I will. By the way, who's the charmer who sent it?"

Pelham answered by opening a note attached to the box which read: "Please accept and enjoy this token of my admiration for 'Gallant Pelham'—from Miss Brill of Orange Court House."

"I suppose you'll want to thank her in person," "Jeb" jested. "My cousin, Nannie Price, is now visiting Miss Brill and can keep an eye on you."

"Sounds like an excellent suggestion, General. I could ride over to inspect Captain Moorman's battery at Orange after which I can call on Miss Brill and your cousin."

"Seeing that Pelham was taking his joke at face value," "Jeb" decided to play along. "Certainly," he said, "I'll have my adjutant issue you an order to inspect Moorman's battery of the Horse Artillery at Orange. You can leave first thing in the morning."

However, Pelham knew from experience that General Stuart often recalled those close to him for companionship. Therefore, the Alabamian rose before dawn and quietly rode off while the staff slept. Later at breakfast, General Stuart noted Pelham's absence, and inquired, "Where's Major Pelham?"

Major Cooke reminded him, "He went to Orange to inspect Moorman's battery."

"Well send a courier and order him to return at once," "Jeb" snapped irritably, annoyed at himself for letting Pelham go.

The courier raced westward across muddy forest trails after Pelham, but he failed to overtake him until evening when they met at Captain Moorman's headquarters just outside of Orange. On reading General Stuart's note, Pelham smiled at the courier and said, "Sergeant, I'm certain that General Stuart wouldn't want me to wear out my horse by riding back over those roads tonight. I'll return first thing tomorrow."

But Pelham's good intentions shortly went awry. That evening as Pelham strolled the streets of Orange with Miss Brill, a group of excited officers hopped off the train arriving from Culpeper. These graycoats, who belonged to General Fitz Lee's cavalry brigade, explained to Pelham that General Averell was massing a large force of Federal cavalry at Kelly's Ford on the Rappahannock. General Fitz Lee had dispatched these aides by train to rush back with a supply of ammunition.

With the enemy preparing to attack General Fitz Lee's force only thirty miles away, Pelham decided on the spot to disregard General Stuart's order to return to Fredericksburg. Instead, he would accompany the ammunition train to Culpeper the following morning. He was sure that "Jeb" would want him to be where he was most needed, and that certainly seemed to be with General Fitz Lee.

When Pelham reached Culpeper he was pleasantly surprised to encounter General Stuart who was in town to testify for an old friend at a court martial. "Jeb" laughingly asked Pelham, "My boy, don't tell me that you have an 'inspection' to make here in Culpeper. Or is there a young beauty that has thrown her net around you?"

Pelham blushed and replied frankly, "General, I must apologize for disobeying your order to return to Camp No-Camp, but when I heard that General Averell is about to attack General Fitz Lee, I thought it best to come here and render what assistance I can."

"You did right, Major," Stuart said approvingly, "the Yankees appear to be heading for Culpeper, but General Fitz Lee has placed 800 troopers across their path at Kelly's Ford. We'll ride out tomorrow and see what's up."

That evening Bessie Shackelford invited Stuart and Pelham to attend a social at her home. After playing a number of classical piano solos, Bessie invited her sisters and the officers to sing various rounds including the familiar "Row, row, row your boat gently down the stream . . ." "Jeb" then led the group through rousing choruses of "Dixie," "Bonnie Blue Flag", "The Yellow Rose of Texas" and other patriotic favorites.

At a late hour the Shackelford belles served coffee and crackers. As Pelham departed, he told Bessie, "I certainly want to thank you for a most enjoyable evening. Tonight you made me forget that there is a war going on. I must leave in the morning, but I'll stop by to wish you happy Saint Patrick's Day."

Tuesday morning, March 17, dawned bright and clear. Major John Pelham rose about 7 o'clock, dressed and buckled on his sword. In the dining room of the Virginia Hotel he ate with General Stuart who reminded him that they would both have to borrow horses to ride to the front."

"I've arranged to borrow Sam Sweeney's rawboned black horse," Pelham replied as he cut his small portion of crisp bacon.

After breakfast, Pelham and Stuart bade farewell to Miss Bessie who stood on her veranda and waved a white lace handkerchief until the two riders disappeared from view. Galloping over the rolling countryside east of Culpeper, the cavalry chief and his companion quickly reached General Fitz Lee's headquarters near the west bank of Kelly's Ford. General Lee reported that just before dawn an enemy squadron had forced its way across the Raappahannock and captured a number of his pickets.

Now, that the bluecoats showed no disposition to advance further, Fitz Lee asked "Jeb": "General, there seem to be only a few platoons in the woods ahead. Don't you think we'd better charge and chase them back across the river?"

"By all means," Stuart agreed. And while General Lee spread out his Third Virginia Cavalry Regiment for a charge, Pelham rode to the rear to assist his old comrade, Captain Jim Breathed, who was struggling to get his four-gun battery into position. As soon as the Blakely guns wheeled out of the mud and into battery, Breathed invited Pelham to sight the guns. Breathed then ordered the crews to fire. The guns blazed and recoiled, drawing an immediate reply from a powerful six-gun enemy battery.

Above the roar of the artillery exchange, Pelham shouted to Breathed, "Keep firing. We must drive them from their position." Then, having no official command or duties on the field, Pelham rode back to the front where General Stuart was rallying the Third Virginia cavalrymen who had fallen back before the deadly fire of Federal sharpshooters to a stone fence that adjoined the road leading from Kelly's Ford. Waving his plumed hat above his head, "Jeb" rode toward the bluecoats and yelled back to his men, "Join me or I'll have to lick the Yankees by myself." Catching his irrepressible spirit, the Virginians turned their horses around and joined in the charge.

As the Third Virginia met the enemy head-on, Tom Rosser led his Second Virginia around the left to assail the stubborn enemy in the flank. Pelham cheered the determined troopers as they charged full-speed into the enemy's ranks. But he was not content to sit idly by and admire his comrades fight valiantly. Instinctively, he drew his saber, and, holding the reins with one hand, he spurred his horse directly into the sword-swinging fray. When he reached the stone fence he rose in his stirrups, turned his head to the troopers following him, and shouted, "Forward! Let's get 'em!"

At that instant a shell exploded on the fence and Pelham toppled from his horse. As he lay stretched face-up on the ground with a smile on his lips and his eyes glassily open, fellow horsemen rushed by certain that he would immediately brush himself off and remount. When he failed to rise, two of Fitz Lee's officers lifted his limp body over the front of the horse—his feet hanging down one side and his out-stretched arms dangling from the other. One of the officers then mounted the charger and cantered to the rear as the enemy staged a counterattack.

After Fitz Lee's veterans repulsed the countercharge and sent the enemy scurrying back across the Rappahannock, word spread that Pelham had been killed. General Stuart was so overcome by this report that he shed tears and exclaimed, "He is irreplaceable."

But despite his rough ride, Pelham was not yet dead. Halfway to Culpeper, one of General Stuart's aides caught up with the horse carrying Pelham's body. Gently removing the motionless form, the officers laid Pelham on the grass beside the road. Although the blood-stained artillerist was unconscious, his heart still beat faintly. Examination revealed that a shell fragment about the size of half a cherry had pierced the back of Pelham's head for a distance of two inches and then emerged without entering the brain. An ambulance was quickly summoned to transport the wounded boy to the Shackelford home

Where Pelham died

where he had enjoyed himself so thoroughly the previous evening. Miss Bessie solicitously bathed and dressed his wound and nestled his head comfortably on a pillow.

General Stuart rushed three surgeons to Pelham's bedside. The medicos were able to relieve the pressure on the wounded boy's neck, but they realized that he could not last the night. With his tremendous vitality, Pelham lingered a few hours without regaining consciousness. Then at one o'clock on Wednesday morning, he opened his eyes, drew a deep breath, and died.

A few moments later, General Stuart, returning from his victory at Kelly's Ford, quietly entered the room where Pelham lay. Hat in hand the great cavalry chief looked down upon the peaceful expression on the face of the lad he loved as a brother. Grief-stricken, "Jeb" simply laid a hand on Pelham's shoulder and uttered the single word, "Farewell."

In his general order to the troops announcing the death of Major John Pelham, General Stuart called on the officers of the cavalry and Horse Artillery to wear the military badge of mourning for thirty days. Major von Borcke was delegated to accompany his dear comrade's remains to Richmond, where Pelham lay in state beneath George Washington's statue in the Capitol. After thousands of mourners paid their last respects to "gallant Pelham", a slow train carried the metal coffin to his native state. Here he was laid to rest in the cemetery at Jacksonville, Alabama.

John Pelham was only twenty-four years old when he died a hero's death. Within the period of a year and a half this youth had organized the Horse Artillery and developed it into a highly mobile arm of the Army of Northern Virginia. General Lee fully recognized Pelham's genius as an artillerist, and paid glowing tribute to him in this message to President Davis:

"I mourn the loss of Major Pelham. I had hoped that a long career of usefulness and honor was still before him. He has been stricken down in the midst of both, and before he could receive the promotion he had richly won. I hope there will be no impropriety in presenting his name to the Senate that his comrades may see that his services have been appreciated, and may be inclined to emulate them."

A grateful Senate, reflecting the South's appreciation, voted Pelham's promotion, and the gallant chief of the Horse Artillery went to his grave with the rank of Lieutenant-Colonel.

Unquestionably, the one who would miss him the most was "Jeb" Stuart. "I loved him as a brother," he wrote Pelham's mother, "he was so noble, so chivalrous, so pure in heart, so beloved." "Jeb" confided to his wife that he hoped their son, Jimmie, would grow up to be just like Pelham. And when the third Stuart child was born in the fall of 1863, "Jeb" named her Virginia Pelham Stuart in honor of the Alabamian.

Colonel John Pelham's notable contribution to military tactics was the development of highly mobile artillery to a degree hitherto unknown. In this field he established the pattern for modern artillery warfare as dashingly exemplified by General Erwin Rommel's tactics in Africa during World War II. Here the "Desert Fox" used mobile 88 millimeter guns with devastating effect in his hit-and-run tactics against the British Eighth Army.

But John Pelham's most enduring and substantial memorial is his exemplary character which inspired his own men to follow anywhere he led, and which challenges subsequent generations to emulate the guileless, handsome youth whose name ever will be synonymous with "gallant."

Monument to Pelham at Jacksonville, Ala.

GLOSSARY

Abolitionist—a person who believed that slavery should be abolished.

Assembly—a signal sounded by a drum or bugle calling the troops to "fall in."

Battery—two or more cannon under a single command. The size of Pelham's batteries varied, but usually consisted of four guns per battery. "Into battery" denotes the placing of guns in firing position.

Bivouac (biv'-wack)—an encampment for a short stay, frequently overnight.

Blakely—a pear-shaped gun made in England and smuggled through the Northern blockade into the Confederacy.

"Boots and Saddles"—a bugle call summoning the cavalrymen to assume their mounted formations.

Caisson (ka-sun')—an ammunition wagon.

Cannoneer—an artillerist who served the guns, i.e.; load, ram, fire or sponge. Eleven cannoneers constituted a full crew for each gun. Two men held the horses while the others served the gun.

Carbine (kar'-bine)—a short rifle or musket especially adapted for cavalry use.

Commissioned officer—any officer having the grade of lieutenant or above who has received a certificate from the government conferring upon him his rank together with its corresponding authority.

Counterattack—an attack made by the defenders upon the attackers after the latter's assault has spent itself.

Courier (koo'-ri-er)—a messenger, normally mounted, who carried dispatches from one commander to another.

Creole—a white person descended from French or Spanish settlers of Louisiana or the Gulf states.

Enfilade (en'-fie-lade)—gunfire directed from the flank along the length of a line of troops.

Fusillade (fu'-zie-lade)—a rapid simultaneous discharge of guns.

Grape—a cluster of nine solid iron balls encased in a shell. (See diagram on page 175.)

Howitzer—a light gun designed to arch shells onto enemy positions as far as a mile away. In appearance it closely resembled the Napoleon gun. (See diagram on page 173.)

Kepi (kep'-e)—the type of cap worn by both Confederate and Union soldiers. It had a flat round top which sloped toward the front visor.

Lanyard (lan'-yerd)—a strong cord attached to a primer, which in turn was buried in the powder charge. When the gunner pulled the lanyard it ignited the primer which then exploded the powder.

Limber (noun)—a chest mounted on a carriage. It contained the tools and ammunition needed in the maintenance and firing of the cannon. Three men usually drove the limber sitting on the left row of a team of six horses. Two other cannoneers rode the chest. In action the limber was placed about ten yards back of the gun. (verb) To hitch the limber to the gun.

Minié ball (min'-ny)—a conical bullet widely used during the Civil War.

Muzzle-loader—a gun that is loaded through the muzzle.

Napoleon gun—this gun, designed by Napoleon III, fired a 12-pound projectile. It had a range of almost a mile. Pelham favored the Napoleon because it was ideally suited for delivering a destructive fire at moderate and close ranges in the wooded, rolling Virginia countryside. (See page 173 for picture of this gun.)

Non-commissioned officer—a subordinate officer having a rank lower than that of a lieutenant. Corporals and sergeants are non-commissioned officers.

Ordnance—military supplies.

Parrott gun—this gun was manufactured across the river from the Academy at West Point. Most of those used by Confederate artillerists were captured in battle. The breech area was reinforced by a thick jacket. The rifled barrel gave it a range of two miles, which made it useful in dueling with enemy artillery at long range. (See page 173 for picture of this gun.)

Pickets—soldiers who stood guard in an advanced line to warn the army of an enemy approach and to dispute any advance against the outposts.

Plebe (pleeb)—a West Point freshman.

Pontoon—a flat-bottomed boat over which planks are laid to construct a pontoon bridge across a river.

Primer (pry'-mer)—a thin tube filled with powder and an igniter which fitted into the gun's vent. It was attached at one end to the lanyard while the other end dug into the powder.

Projectile—missiles fired from cannon. Grape, cannister, solid, and case projectiles were employed by artillerists during the Civil War. Solid shot was simply a solid iron ball. Case shot or shrapnel consisted of round musket-balls packed into a hollow iron ball. A 12-pounder spherical case shell contained approximately 80 bullets. (See page 175 for diagrams of various projectiles.)

Ration—a daily food allowance issued to each soldier. Before a battle enough provisions to last several days were distributed for each soldier to cook and carry with him into battle so that he wouldn't have to take time out during the fighting to prepare his meal. However, the underfed Confederate soldier frequently consumed his extra ration as soon as he had cooked it.

Reveille (rev'-ee-ly)—a bugle or drum call to awaken soldiers early in the morning.

Ricochet (rick'-o-shay)—to rebound or glance off an object.

Rifled gun—a cannon whose barrel is grooved to impart a rotary motion to the projectile thereby resulting in greater accuracy. The Blakely and Parrott guns were rifled.

Round of ammunition—one shot per gun. Ten rounds of ammunition means that there is enough ammunition available for each gun to shoot ten times.

Salvo—a discharge of shot by guns firing either simultaneously or in series.

Secessionist—a person who believed that the states should withdraw from the Union.

Sentinel—a guard or sentry who guards the camp.

Six-pounder—a six-pound projectile. A six-pounder gun is one which fires six-pound projectiles.

Smooth bore—a plain, ungrooved muzzle. The Napoleon and howitzer were smooth-bore cannon.

Sorrel—a reddish-brown horse.

Sponger—a cannoneer who swabbed the muzzle of a cannon with a wet spongestaff to extinguish any sparks that might remain after the gun had been fired.

Spongestaff—a long pole attached to a sponge—(a wooden cylinder covered with bristles or lambskin.) (See sketch on page 174.)

Sutler—during the Civil War an army of merchants filled wagons with provisions which they sold to troops on the march and in camp. Often they stocked luxury items such as dried fruit and ginger cakes which they sold at fancy prices.

Taps—a bugle call which notified the soldiers to turn out all lights and go to bed.

Tether—to allow a horse to graze and move about at the end of a rope which is fastened at the other end to a post.

Twelve-pounder—a twelve-pound projectile. A twelve-pound gun fired a twelve-pound projectile.

Unlimber—to unfasten or unhitch the horses from the limber. The term is commonly used to indicate the unhitching of any two objects.

Vidette (vid-et')—a mounted sentinel.

Whitworth gun—a rifled, long-range (3-4 miles) gun made in England.

INSIDE A LOADED CANNON

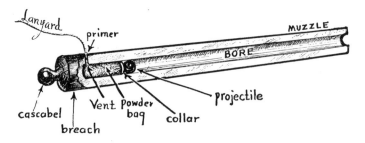

TYPES OF GUNS USED BY PELHAM

NAPOLEON

PARROTT

BLAKELY

CAISSON AND LIMBER

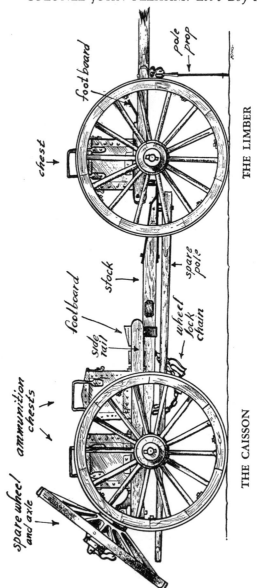

pole prop

footboard

chest

THE LIMBER

stock

spare pole

footboard

wheel lock chain

side rail

ammunition chests

THE CAISSON

spare wheel and axle

GUNNERY TOOLS

HANDSPIKE

A large bar used to move the carriage and lift the breech of the gun so that the elevating screw could be adjusted.

RAMMER

A wooden cylinder having a diameter about the same as the shot. It pushed or "rammed" the ammunition firmly into the gun.

WORMER

This corkscrew-like piece was inserted into the gun bore and twisted so as to catch and remove any wads and residue left by the cartridge bags after firing.

SPONGE

A wooden cylinder about a foot long covered with lambskin or bristles. It was mounted on a long pole (spongestaff). After dipping the sponge in water, the cannoneer plunged it into the bore to extinguish any sparks which might set off the next charge prematurely. The vent was closed by thumb during sponging to prevent sparks from gathering in the vent and exploding the next charge as it was being loaded. The sponge also helped to clean the bore and cool the gun. Sometimes the sponge was attached to the opposite end of the rammer.

GUNNER'S PICK

A sharp pointed tool that was rammed down the vent to pierce the powder bag so that the flame from the primer could ignite the charge.

 TOMPION

A lid that fitted over the mouth of the muzzle when the gun was not in use. A lead cover was placed over the vent to prevent moisture and weathering from deteriorating the gun.

TYPES OF AMMUNITION

ROUND SHOT

This projectile was useful in knocking out enemy batteries.

BOMBS OR SHELLS

A bombshell was a hollow cast-iron sphere filled with powder. It was used in general bombardments. A delayed action shell with a time fuse spread consternation as it rolled among enemy troops.

SPHERICAL CASE OR SHRAPNEL

A shell filled with bullets and fitted with a time fuse which exploded the shell in the air, spraying bullets over a wide area.

CASE OR CANISTER

This projectile consisted of a can or case filled with musket balls, slugs, or scrap. It was used to pepper the enemy at close range.

GRAPE SHOT

This projectile consisted of a cluster of iron balls (larger than those in canister) mounted on a wooden base and bagged in cloth reinforced with cords. It was more effective at long range than canister.

GUNNERY PRACTICE AND OPERATION

GUNNER AND CANNONEERS AT ATTENTION

Sponging *Serving vent* *Gunner sighting*

SERVING THE GUN

GUNNERY OPERATIONS

SUGGESTIONS FOR FURTHER READING

R. S. Henry, *The Story of the Confederacy,* Grosset and Dunlap.

C. Dowdey, *The Land They Fought For,* Doubleday.

J. C. Wise, *The Long Arm of Lee,* Oxford.

P. Mercer, *The Life of The Gallant Pelham,* Continental Book Company.

C. G. Milham, *Gallant Pelham,* Public Affairs Press.

W. T. Poague, *Gunner With Stonewall,* McCowat-Mercer Press, Inc.

K. Douglas, *I Rode With Stonewall,* U. of North Carolina Press.

W. W. Blackford, *War Years With Jeb Stuart,* Scribners.

G. M. Neese, *Three Years in the Confederate Horse Artillery.* This book, published in 1911, is out of print and will have to be obtained through a large public library. Neese did not serve with Pelham, but his account provides a vivid picture of life in the horse artillery.

F. Downey, *The Guns At Gettysburg,* McKay.

B. Davis, *Jeb Stuart The Last Cavalier,* Rinehart.

J. W. Thomason, Jr., *Jeb Stuart.*

E. S. Miers, *Billy Yank and Johnny Reb: How They Fought and Made Up,* Rand-McNally.

Albert Manucy, *Artillery Through The Ages.* This excellent pamphlet may be obtained for thirty-five cents from the Superintendent of Documents, U. S. Government Printing Office, Washington 25, D. C. It is packed with information and diagrams and provides a history of cannon with emphasis on the types used in America.

INDEX